Praise for
DEVELOPING PEOPLE
By Arnauld de Nadaillac

This book is a testament to Arnauld's 35+ years of expertise in human resources development across 14 countries, in which he weaves personal experiences and global insights, inviting readers on a journey of self-reflection and experiential learning.

—Dr Libing Wang, Chief, Section for Educational Innovation and Skills Development (EISD),
UNESCO Multisectoral Regional Office in Bangkok

What sets Arnauld's book apart is not only its wealth of knowledge but also his ability to present complex concepts in a simple and engaging manner. His writing is clear, concise and filled with real-life examples and case studies that resonate with readers. Moreover, his passion for helping others shines through every page, making it an inspiring and motivating read for anyone interested in HRD.

—Manoon Sunkunakorn, Corporate HR Advisor

This is a rare opportunity to gain an insight into the construction of recognized expertise, based on an ongoing self-reflection on a long and rich experience in HRD.

—Alexandre Berthon-Dumurgier, Agence Francaise de Développement,
Technical, Vocational, Skills Development Advisor

This book is an excellent learning experience for me and for everyone interested in working in Human Resources Development. It shows the clear journey on HRD strategies based on practical experiences.

—Dr Siripan Choomnoom, Chair of Public & Private Committee on International
Cooperation, Office of Vocational Education, Ministry of Education, Thailand

Arnauld has a passion for people development that can support any businesses like he has done for us in Thailand. Through this book you will be able to discover the rich and fascinating experience of an HR expert.

A book to read, with a very professional and transparent approach, from Arnauld robust Human Resources Development experience.

Arnauld's personal stories, practical examples, tips, and concepts demonstrate his deep professional insights, collaborative approach, cross cultural awareness and customer centricity. His book is a must-read for any manager or leader who's passionate about human resource development!

DEVELOPING PEOPLE

35 YEARS OF STORIES, HEADACHES AND INSIGHTS

ARNAULD DE NADAILLAC

CONTENTS

Introduction   vii

Gratitude   ix

Part 1: Sharing Principles and Visions of Efficient Learning and Development   1

1. Learning Methods are Changing ... Finally   3
2. Start With the End in Mind   11
3. Navigating Competency Systems: What Wind to Follow?   19
4. My Lifelong Self-Development   27
5. Leaders Are Important: But How to Develop Them?   35
6. Disruption In Learning Systems: How to Avoid Being a Dinosaur   43
7. From Offline to Online Training: Headaches and Medicines   53

Part 2: How to Implement Hrd Systems?   59

8. Transferring New Hrd Systems But Making Them Sustainable   61
9. Future-Proof Production Operators and Workers   69
10. So Many Kinds of Customers or Potential Ones   77
11. Matching Training Demands and Needs   83
12. Getting Business and Education to Speak a Common Language   91
13. Vocational Education Systems: How to Succeed With Improvement   99

**Part 3: Knowledge, Skills, and Capacities Needed
to Successfully Implement These Systems**

Part 3: ... 107

14. Skills Needed to Keep My Job   109

15. Culture Shock: Managing Cross-Cultural Differences   117

16. Leading a Team Of Consultants: Challenging But Exciting   125

17. Avoiding Being Lost in Translation   133

18. Facts, Feelings, and Opinions: The Communication Trinity   139

19. How it All Started   145

20. Conclusion: Key Learnings and Concepts   151

INTRODUCTION

Welcome!

It all started back in 2020. Like many people all over the world, the COVID-19 period was, for me, a time of self-reflection. I had almost reached 60, was close to having 35 years of experience in people development (training, teaching, and consulting), and had been living in Thailand for 25 years.

Over the course of my career, I have had difficulties, failures, challenges, stress; but also feelings of satisfaction, successful projects, memorable relations, and so on, as everyone does. And it is still ongoing (I just hope there are less failures in the future ...).

During my training sessions, workshops or meetings, I frequently draw from my personal experiences, and at one point, I thought: "Why not formalize this informal ("tacit") knowledge?"

I believe that we need to set ourselves personal objectives to succeed. Thus, I started by setting the goal of publishing two articles per month on LinkedIn over the course of one year.

I surprised myself by succeeding in this first challenge.

I then decided to consolidate all these articles into a book but it took me a while to really get started.

All the chapters of this book follow the same structure: connecting personal stories and experience to key concepts and learnings. There are some academic references, but I purposely tried to focus on reality rather than theory.

I tried to illustrate all these key concepts with drawings and symbols; it helps me to give structure to the knowledge that I gained.

Here are some examples of key learnings from my life that I share in this book:

♦ Realizing that I liked education when I was teaching in a Moroccan school.

♦ Learning about Asian cultural subtleties when creating a training center on sewing-machine repair in a Thai refugee camp.

♦ Discovering the learner-centered training method when I was working, as a young consultant, in a French training institute with colleagues who had more than 20 years' experience in experiential learning and participative pedagogies.

♦ Diving into competency-based systems thanks to an exciting Thai-French cooperation project.

♦ Understanding how learning can be driven by evaluation after I gained two US and UK certifications on how to measure the return on investment of HRD programs.

♦ Experiencing the importance of being strategic and flexible when I developed vocational education and HRD in countries as different as the Republic of Marshall Islands and Bangladesh.

I hope you will enjoy this book and its stories and, even more so, that the principles, concepts, and key learnings shared will be useful for you.

Shall we dive in?

GRATITUDE

Numerous individuals have played pivotal roles in shaping the person I am today, both on personal and professional levels.

I refrain from mentioning their names to protect their privacy as they have worked or are currently employed by the following organizations:

- The French association Ecoles Sans Frontières and the CESI institute which have both determined my professional orientation.
- Companies, organizations and institutes with whom I had great projects over the course of several years: King Mongkut's University of Technology North Bangkok, the French Embassy to Thailand, the Federation of Thai Industries, the Office of Vocational Education (OVEC), Siam Cement Group (SCG), Bouygues Construction (special mention to Bouygues-Thai), EssilorLuxottica, Thainamthip, Dextra Group, Parex Group, Hypertrade Consulting, VT Garment, Krungthai Bank, NTPC (Laos), Archetype.
- International development partners which trusted me to work on one or several memorable assignments: Asian Development Bank, UNESCO Bangkok, International Labour Organization (Bangkok office), SFERE (France), ICON Institute

> (Germany), Agence Française de Développement, The
> Deutsche Gesellschaft für Internationale Zusammenarbeit
> GmbH (GIZ), Swiss Development Cooperation.
> - Consulting partners I learnt with: TaF.tc (Singapore), Sofreco
>   (France), KRIVET (Korea), Opifer (Finland), TRA-C Industries
>   (France), ABDI (UK), Hifab (Sweden).
> - National organizations and ministries of Bangladesh,
>   Cambodia, Georgia, Lao PDR, Marshall Islands, Sri Lanka,
>   Uzbekistan, Vietnam.

Special thanks to my daughter Yanie, Andrew Dawson and Glen Edelstein who reviewed drafts of this book and brought their expertise for edition and design.

And I am also grateful to …

My wife, Nipa, who always supported my professional decisions despite the stress they caused, who accepts my frequent trips abroad, and who is a constant support both at home and with work, all while running her own successful career.

My two children, Yanie and Loïc, with whom I share this exciting life. I thoroughly enjoy hearing about their professional journeys and discussing their successes, difficulties, and uncertainties.

PART 1:

SHARING PRINCIPLES AND VISIONS OF EFFICIENT LEARNING AND DEVELOPMENT

1. LEARNING METHODS ARE CHANGING ... FINALLY

What do the production of cars, chairs, and clothes have in common?

Over the course of the last century, the manufacturing processes have completely changed: new machines, more automation, and evolving management methods have brought higher efficiency, productivity, quality, innovation, and safety.

Yet, the basic process of how we acquire our knowledge and skills hasn't really changed for thousands of years. From the moment we are born, and throughout our professional life, teachers speak and learners listen; maybe put into action what they have been told; and, hopefully, learn something (that they may or may not subsequently forget). It has been this way for more than 2,000 years. It's mind-blowing, when you think about it. Why do we still have such an outdated method for transferring knowledge when the way we produce goods has changed so drastically?

Let me share three situations demonstrating this lack of evolution.

1. Education

Since graduating with my Master of Engineering in 1984, I have always wondered about my schools' pedagogy.

Over the five-year course, the same teaching method was applied again and again: lectures in big groups and then exercises and practice sessions in small groups. Projects and internships were the only change from the daily "chalk and talk" method.

There was no specific learning approach and no originality in teaching. The only teachers I remember were those good at public speaking or ones whose comments demotivated me.

It seems to me that most higher education schools and universities follow the same format. I don't know any friend or colleague my age who can tell me that they love their past school or university because of its interesting pedagogy or teaching approach. Any sense of belonging to our educational institution mainly came from its reputation, the level of difficulty to enter it, and, more often than not, the great fun we had *outside* the lecture room.

You might tell me that things have changed since my time as a student in the '80s but, based on my readings and discussions with my children, I don't see any significant pedagogical change, nor many revolutions driven by policy-makers.

In Thailand, where I now live, it is no better. Thai culture puts a big emphasis on respect for older people, with a clear sense of hierarchy. In the context of education and training, students are careful not to ask their teachers questions to ensure that they don't lose face in case they can't answer them. For more than 20 years while living in this country, I have heard and read about the need to change the teaching method. There have been more than 20 ministers of education in 20 years, and all of them mention the need to change the teaching method. But none of them have been successful; it's not easy to develop a participative pedagogy in a culture based on respect of the hierarchy.

2. Professional training

I first encountered this deferential dynamic between teacher and learner when I started to be a trainer in Thailand. In France, whenever I was doing training sessions, at the end of activities, the debriefing with participants was always very interactive, filled with comments and questions. So, when I moved to Thailand, nearly 30 years ago, I started using the same approach, asking questions such as, "What do you think went well? What did you notice in this simulation?" And nobody spoke. The debriefing would be over in 30 seconds. It was rather awkward, to say the least. Since then, I have adapted my approach. Whenever I need to get feedback from participants, I no longer ask open questions. I "force" them to speak by giving a precise assignment: "Write on a piece of paper the three questions you have," or, "List the main strengths and weaknesses of this presentation in order to improve it," or, "Fill in this questionnaire."

You might say that it was a long time ago, but nothing has changed since then. I still need to use the same methods to make trainees express their opinions.

A few years ago, as I was preparing a training program for internal trainers in an international company selling construction materials, their HR manager told me with great conviction, "Arnauld, I think that the most important competency of a good trainer is to speak well."

I replied, "Sir, I'm sorry, but the most important competency of a good trainer is to listen well. This means listening to the trainees' needs, their experience, their feelings, and their motivation."

The HR manager could not see what I meant. Still now, the message is clear: In many training courses, the trainer is called the "speaker."

3. Capacity-building programs in international projects

When improving training and education systems across the world, I team up with experts in various areas (i.e., finance, procurement, technical) to implement large, multi-million-dollar projects. This includes building capacity and training local government staff, teachers, and managers. We are hired by international development partners, and thus local governments assume that these experts have the competencies needed to train others because they have recognized knowledge in their areas. This dated and persistent belief is found everywhere in the world.

I was once in a team of international experts tasked with planning how to spend a $100 million budget to strengthen the vocational education system in an Asian country. One of the experts was in charge of building capacity for the ministry staff's labor market information system. He listed a series of one- or two-day training sessions for groups of 50 participants, without specific recommendations on the training method that should be used. While I understand that planning the training of hundreds of teachers and managers is extremely challenging, I couldn't help but think, *how can we train 50 people efficiently in two days? This expert with more than 30 years of experience seems to have never been trained on pedagogy; maybe he doesn't know that he doesn't know pedagogy?*

In another project, we had to plan 17 training programs for thousands of teachers and school managers. I wrote to the project manager, "We did not mention specific recommendations for the training method, and we know that learners forget 75% of what they were taught within three days. What will be the mechanisms to ensure that the training will be effective?" He accepted my point of view, and we defined modalities ensuring that learning gained from training would be applied at work so it would not be a waste of money.

The capacity-building model that development partners and organizations use or recommend is often no different from the model used in higher education. They often don't understand that the best technical expert can be the worst trainer or training program designer. The capacity to design and implement a training program is a skill that needs to be learned. Many of these international organizations or ministries don't have a vision of efficient pedagogical concepts that could be applied by the hired experts. Consequently, those being trained don't apply much of the knowledge learned to their work, so money is being wasted because new systems are not being implemented as they should be.

These are just a few examples of situations where the pedagogies[1] and methods we use to transfer knowledge, whether to a 20-year-old student or

---

1 I use the more common term "pedagogy," but technically, as we are talking about adult learners only, it should be "andragogy," which the *Cambridge Dictionary* defines as, "The theory, methods, and activities involved in teaching adult learners."

a 50-year-old engineer, have failed to continuously improve in the same way we have developed our methods for producing cars, chairs, or machines.

In fact, throughout history, great thinkers, educators, philosophers, and researchers have promoted new pedagogical approaches. Yet, those have not always been passed on and adopted.

Nearly 2,500 years ago (yes, it's been a while), Greek philosopher Socrates encouraged people to question the things they were told to improve and learn, which is still considered an innovative approach in many education and training organizations.

Starting from the early 20th century onwards, various researchers supported the evolution of pedagogy. Lev S. Vygotsky, a Soviet psychologist, promoted new pedagogical approaches through actions and relationships. Later, American philosopher and educator John Dewey developed the idea that all students should have the opportunity to take part in their own learning. Meanwhile, Italian physician and educator Maria Montessori emphasized students' independence. Swiss psychologist Jean Piaget highlighted the importance of exploration and pleasure in child development. Célestin Freinet, a French pedagogue and educator, developed inquiry-based learning and the pedagogy of work. Similarly, Paulo Freire, an educator and philosopher from Brazil, focused on adult learning based on questioning and awareness. More recently, Seymour Papert promoted the problem-solving approach in pedagogy and English teacher and educator Paul Ginnis summarized how neuroscience can support learning.

As you can see, many people have been thinking a lot about the process of learning and how to improve it.

Based on this research and more than 30 years of experience in HRD, I sum up below nine principles (with their academic sources) that I try to implement in my projects:

1. **Learning design**

    Learning is a process: Analyze needs/Design program/Develop materials/Implement training/Evaluate and adjust (ADDIE, Robert Gagne).

2. **Starting with the end in mind**

    As learners, we want to answer two questions: What is the expected impact of the program? (Jack Phillips, Donald Kirkpatrick) and what learning objectives are we going to achieve? (Benjamin Bloom)

3. **Motivation drivers**

    We want to connect new learning to existing knowledge and experience (constructionism). We look for relevance in relation to the future, clarity on the reason for learning (why?), how it can be applied in the future, and autonomy (Malcom Knowles).

4. **Learning activities**

    We need to practice, apply theory, conceptualize theories, and reflect (cognitivism and David A. Kolb).

5. **Learning by doing**

    We remember 10% of what we read and 90% if we train others (William Glasser).

6. **Attention span**

    Our attention span when listening to a speech is around 20 minutes (that's why TED Talks rarely last any longer!).

7. **Challenges and emotions**

    We remember better if we are focused, challenge our brain, and experience emotions (neurosciences).

8. **Spaced repetition**

    We forget 80% of what we learn three days after learning it (Hermann Ebbinghaus). That is why we need repetition and reward (behaviorism).

9. **Learning styles**
    We need to mix visual, auditory, reading/writing, kinesthetic learning approaches (VARK model, Walter Burke Barbe and Neil Fleming).

All these principles enable us to learn, remember, and apply.

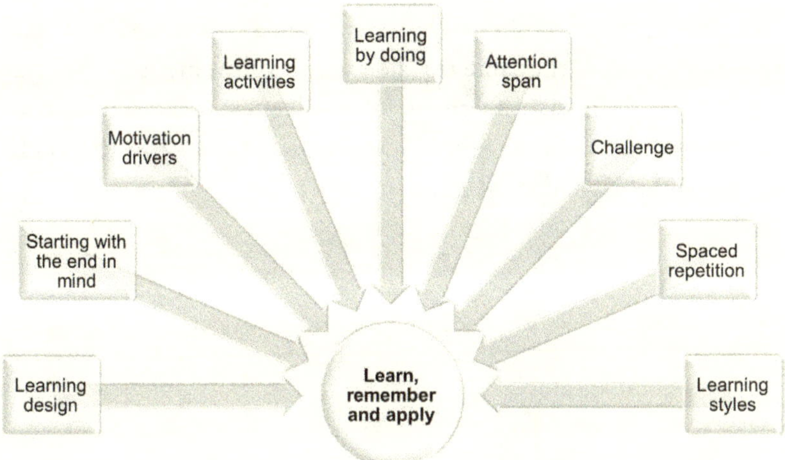

Figure 1.1: Nine principles to learn, remember, and apply

Conclusion

These principles are very comprehensive, and I try to apply them as much as possible.

And I am not the only one; things have started to change.

After more than 2,000 years of very little development of teaching and training methods, innovations have been gradually coming in the past 20 years; and this process is accelerating –the opportunities are endless with the advent of artificial intelligence.

New technologies, competition in the educational and training market, the need to measure the return on investment of training programs, and the recent impact of the COVID-19 crisis are bringing changes in teaching and training. At last!

We hear about initiatives and methods such as flipped classrooms, learning by doing, blended learning (e.g., digital content with traditional classroom sessions), project-based learning, community of practice, mentoring, micro-learning, action-learning, the metaverse, learning management systems, artificial intelligence, to mention a few.

So maybe, finally, the way we "produce" educated and skilled people might follow the same trajectory of improvement as the one we have observed in the manufacturing of goods such as cars or electronics.

In this book, I will share how I apply these pillars to various HRD programs and the challenges I face.

2. START WITH THE END IN MIND

This is one of the nine principles, described in the first chapter, that I try to use when implementing learning and development programs. It is where I should begin if I want to be true to my word of focusing on the end result.

Defining expectations when it comes to the development of people has always been very challenging for two main reasons: 1) Knowledge and skills cannot be as easily quantified as cars or computers; 2) Everyone is different. People's experience, education, background, and culture will determine how much they learn and how they apply it. So, how can I evaluate the results of my HRD programs for companies or governments?

1. Evaluating training programs in companies

In 2013, an HR manager told me, "Arnauld, I appreciate you helping my HR teams become better trainers. Thanks to you, they know how to use the learner-centered method and how to build competency-based training. Now, I would like you to train my team to evaluate the impact, the efficiency, and the financial impact of the training we organized within our company."

At first, I was a bit confused and not sure what he wanted, but I quickly realized that this kind of question was increasingly asked by decision-makers in companies. That meant that I needed to develop my evaluation skills so that I could give clear, relevant, in-depth answers.

There began my quest. I did some research on existing methods and tools, then went to the UK to complete a certification program (Pearson level 5) on how to measure the efficiency of training and its return on investment based on the Jack Phillips methodology.[2] I also got certified on the same method by the ROI Institute in the USA one year later.

Since then, I have used five levels of evaluation to determine the success of HR development programs:

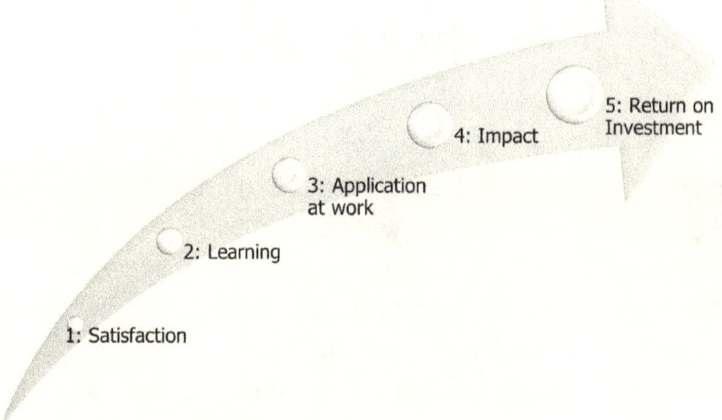

Figure 2.1: Five levels of evaluation

- Level 1: At the end of the training session, we evaluate the satisfaction of trainees on the training (content, method, training room, etc.) and their motivation to implement new skills and knowledge. It can be done through simple questionnaires.
- Level 2: During or at the end of the training session, we evaluate the new knowledge and skills gained through tests/quizzes, observation, role play, or presentations (e.g., the training on negotiation skills will end with a small quiz on the negotiation process and a negotiation simulation).
- Level 3: Several weeks after the training session, we evaluate the change of, usually, three to seven precise

---

2 https://roiinstitute.net/

behaviors or competencies at work (e.g., planning work based on the motivation and skills of the team members, giving corrective feedback, repairing a mechanical system). To do so, we can use questionnaires, observations, real situations, or projects.

- ♦ Level 4: Several months after the training session, we evaluate the impact of these new behaviors on defined indicators, then quantify this as revenue using available monetary data. There are seven main indicators of impact:
  - ♦ Time saved
  - ♦ Cost saved
  - ♦ Number of outputs, results, production, productivity (e.g., monthly sales, number of car parts or electrical components produced per day, etc.)
  - ♦ Level of quality
  - ♦ Working atmosphere inside the organization
  - ♦ Level of customer satisfaction
  - ♦ Number of innovations
- ♦ Level 5: We calculate the total cost of the training, both direct expenses (trainer fees, training room rent, lunch and lodging of participants, training materials, etc.) and indirect ones, especially the time spent by the participants on the training. Comparing this cost to the revenue identified at level 4, we can calculate the benefits, or return on investment (ROI).

Before calculating the ROI, it is essential at level 4 to *isolate* the direct benefits of the program compared to other possible effects (change of organization, manager, economic situation, etc.). You could do this by comparing the data with groups of people who have not participated in the intervention (control group), interviewing experts, or by looking at trends in other departments or companies which have implemented the training methods previously.

Not all programs are evaluated at level 5. Usually, companies measure ROI in this way for around 10% of programs because producing reliable data and the corresponding analysis take time and require a very good knowledge of the evaluation method and tools.

Using these clear guidelines, I can evaluate the impact of training programs at various levels depending on the needs of the organization. In the specific case of soft-skills training, I recommend evaluating to at least level 3 (change of behaviors at work) because there can be big gap between knowing the theory (e.g., identify the conditions to be a good coach), and applying this at work (e.g., coach team members at work. Putting the theory into practice is more difficult when it comes to soft skills compared to functional or technical skills like programming a computer or preparing a financial statement. Moreover, soft skills are often too broadly defined (e.g., "develop leadership skills"), with the consequence that they cannot be evaluated at work. Writing them precisely and evaluating them at level 3 (new behaviors), level 4 (impact), or level 5 (ROI) is essential.

Thanks to these interventions, I have also learned how important it is to use quantitative data from systematic data collections at all levels.

Below are some real-life examples of how I used these levels of evaluation.

The HR director of a large Thai conglomerate once asked me to audit a program supporting student internships in their factories. He thought this program was relatively cost-effective at $200,000 per year for seminars, meetings, allowance, and transportation of students. My first audit conclusion shocked him: data showed that, in fact, the program cost the company $600,000! He forgot to include all the time spent by his engineers to train, advise, and monitor students every day.

In another case, a banking company asked me to analyze the efficiency of a two-day leadership training session they had organized for their supervisors with a well-known training center. As a pre-test before the session, the training center sent a questionnaire listing 39 leadership behaviors to the managers of the supervisors. They had to tick any behaviors displayed by their subordinates, such as "creates a culture that attracts high performers" or "genuinely listens to others." They sent the same questionnaire after the session. The results were eye-opening. Before the training, the managers believed their subordinates displayed 89% of the leadership behaviors (100% meant that their subordinates demonstrated the behavior perfectly). After training, the number fell to 85% – yes, the score after training was lower than before! I told them that the training should have focused on far fewer expected behavior changes so the trainees and their manager could concentrate more on key areas.

We evaluated the ROI of a sales training module at the same bank. This time, there was a positive impact:

1. Questionnaires showed that trainees were satisfied.
2. The small tests and simulations proved that they integrated new learnings.
3. Three months after the training, the questionnaires sent to their managers and the self-assessments confirmed the change of behaviors.
4. There was a significant increase in sales turnover six months after the training, a change that was confirmed when compared with a control group of managers who did not follow the training.
5. An ROI analysis showed that for every $100 invested in training, the company gained $185 (based on sales results from the first year after training).

Here's another example which shows the importance of identifying precise behaviors. A pharmaceutical company asked me to prepare and implement an evaluation system after sessions of action learning. The sales HRD manager told me, "We want to develop communication skills." From this broad scope, we identified a set of specific situations so participants could focus on precise skills. For example, asking questions based on prepared guidelines when visiting doctors. In this way, we were able to identify behavior changes through the evaluation process.

I like this precise approach, but, for the implementation of this method to be a total success, I also need certain conditions: 1) The impact indicators should be defined before the beginning of the program; 2) The expected new behaviors must be precise and only of a limited number; 3) Data on the evaluation results at each level is available and the tools used ensure credibility; 4) The isolation techniques are implemented precisely.

In Thailand, I face one main challenge that jeopardizes the credibility of the results. When asked to provide opinions on the level of applications at work or impact, Thai trainees and/or their managers tend to be too "nice" in their opinion in order to keep the reviewer happy (and not lose face!). Therefore, I might end up with very good scores. I try to mitigate this risk by asking precise questions and obtaining various proofs (data) to guarantee the credibility of the method.

2. Evaluating large projects, including HRD components

I have also had the opportunity to use another guideline to evaluate large projects implemented by international organizations and development partners (e.g., European Union, Asian Development Bank, International Labour Organization) which are not only about people development. This other approach has a wider scope, taking into account the following six criteria:

Relevance	• Are the activities designed to achieve the outcomes and outputs planned at the beginning?
Coherence	• How well does the intervention fit into the local context?
Effectiveness	• Is the intervention achieving its objectives?
Efficiency	• How well are resources being used?
Impact	• What difference does the intervention make?
Sustainability	• Will the benefits last?

Figure 2.2: Six criteria to evaluate projects

In this situation, evaluation intervention is important and involves the collection of various types of data.

I implemented this kind of evaluation for the cooperation agency of a country that wanted to evaluate an $8 million program supporting migration through capacity building, skills development, counseling, and assistance to migrant workers from Lao PDR, Cambodia, and Myanmar heading to Thailand.

For each criterion, we defined a list of questions adapted to the way the program had been defined and implemented. With a team of four consultants, we produced a 20-page report based on 80 meetings (individual and focus group discussions) with stakeholders (representatives of the operating agency, beneficiaries, partners, suppliers, etc.) and reviewed 130 reports and documents. The purpose was to get data and opinions that provided a set of proofs to allow us to give an opinion on each criterion with confidence.

This evaluation model can be applied to HR development programs and any other kinds of intervention meant to develop a system, an organization, or even a country. It is very comprehensive, but there are three challenges:

1. When an overwhelming amount of data is involved, it must be cross-checked to ensure synthesis.
2. The opinions expressed by the stakeholders must be challenged in interviews (which can sometimes bring about tense situations).
3. The writing of the final report takes a lot of time as each word is important, especially when the contractor wants brevity (in the case mentioned above, my customer asked me to write a 20-page report, which was a very challenging task).

If I want to connect this second model with the five-levels guide presented before, I would say that levels 1 (satisfaction), 2 (learning), and 3 (new behavior) correspond to "effectiveness" and level 4 (impact) relates to "sustainability," "relevance," and "impact." Level 5 corresponds to "efficiency."

Conclusion

With these two tools, the five-level HRD evaluation grid and the six-criteria project evaluation, I should feel comfortable about evaluating the process of HR development.

However, things are changing. It's not as easy as it may seem anymore.

Why? Because learning is no longer about a three-day training session with 15 people in a room. The future of learning is said to be ATAWAD: anytime, anywhere, any device. HR development projects are less and less a fixed program with precise activities. Nowadays, learning is increasingly integrated into daily life through many modalities, such as project-based learning, micro-learning, podcasts, e-learning, and social media, as future chapters will show.

So how can I evaluate the efficiency of learning using the five-level grid or six-criteria evaluation model when the definition of learning itself is changing, when the future of learning is to be more and more integrated and diluted into both our personal and professional lives?

If we cannot evaluate the results easily, then we need to ensure that the process supports sustainable learning and behavior change. In the next chapters, we will deep dive into various learning processes and identify conditions to succeed using real examples, principles, and concepts.

3. NAVIGATING COMPETENCY SYSTEMS: WHAT WIND TO FOLLOW?

The goal of learning and development is ultimately to improve existing behaviors at work or acquire new ones. Therefore, if we want to "start with the end in mind," as mentioned in the previous chapter, we need to implement a *competency-based learning approach*, ensuring that the training modules or programs are based on the expected learning outcomes and competencies needed in the workplace.

Competencies are mentioned in every business book, every HR development manual, and every recruitment brochure. But what exactly are they? How do we define competency?

A Thai organization once asked me to run training on competency systems, expecting that a foreigner would have *the* "good" western model.

That is not what happened. Instead of giving them one model, I asked the participants to compare five different models of competency systems that I had implemented in Asia and to review their strengths and potential issues.

After discussing, the consensus was clear: They were confused.

"So then ... there isn't one good model, is there?" they asked, scratching their heads.

"Indeed, there isn't *one* good competency system. There are 12 definitions from 12 different researchers on Wikipedia alone!" I replied.

I often use the drawing below to define competency. From the various academic definitions that can be found in many HR books, I summarize it as the capacity to apply knowledge, skills, and attributes in a working situation.

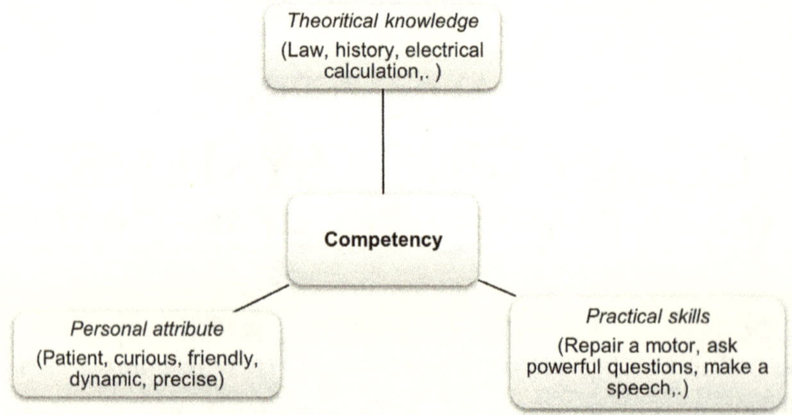

Figure 3.1: Components of a competency

So how do we navigate all the different competency models and find the right one for our project?

First, let us remember the purpose. Why are competencies so important for companies and governments?

Companies seek to identify, use, and evaluate their staff's competencies (knowledge and skills) in order to support their training, career path, recruitment, and/or salary scale.

Government institutions include competencies in the national degree or diploma they award at the end of people's studies. So, an official document clearly states that they are now able to, for example, repair electrical motors, lead a team, negotiate, prepare a business plan, or sell a product.

I found during all these years working on HRD that there are several models used to define and structure competencies.

At the *national* level, different countries have different approaches:

- In the UK and some other European and Asian countries, competency refers to the performance of fragmented and narrowly-defined tasks split in units, elements, criteria, and knowledge.[3] For example, the unit of competency "use social media to engage customers" has four elements of competency (e.g., "prepare to use social media") and 19 performance criteria (e.g., "review organizational social media requirements and policies and procedures.")[4] Programs and certifications are based on the addition of these units.

- In France, competency is broadly defined as the use of knowledge, know-how, and attributes in various situations for a professional activity.[5] France has developed the concept of a "block of competencies," that is those that always go together and can't be split. For example, to be an HR assistant, you will need to have four blocks of competencies corresponding to the four key areas of this position: administration, recruitment, management of compensation and benefits, and recruitment.

- Similarly, in Germany, the term competency is generally used to describe the accumulated knowledge, capabilities, and skills of individuals which enable them to master specific tasks.[6]

- Sometimes, within the same country, different ministries don't even agree on the common method to define competencies (this is often the case for the ministries of education and labor).

At the *international* level, the International Labour Organization defines competencies in a similar way to the UK, based on units and elements. They are promoted in Asia under a regional model of competency standards.[7]

---

3 Brockmann, M., Clark, L., Méhaut, P., & Winch, C. (2008) Competence-based vocational education and training (VET): the cases of England and France in a European perspective, Vocations and Learning, 1 (3), pp. 227-244
4 https://training.gov.au/Training/Details/ICTSS00108
5 https://www.francecompetences.fr/
6 https://cumulus.cedefop.europa.eu/files/vetelib/2016/ReferNet_DE_KC.pdf
7 https://www.ilo.org/asia/publications/WCMS_496514/lang--en/index.htm

Companies in Thailand (and many other countries) do not use these kinds of definitions, with units and elements like in the UK or in blocks like in France, but often adopt the so-called American approach. In this case, each competency is given a general definition declined in descriptors or behaviors at different levels. In the US, the Society for Human Resource Management (SHRM) competencies are defined at four levels: early level, mid-level, senior level, and executive level. For example, leadership is defined by "the ability to direct and contribute to initiatives and processes within the organization." This competency has an overall description of nine associated behaviors (e.g., foster collaboration) and is declined in each level with more than 10 proficiency standards (e.g., for the early level, "build credibility with stakeholders").

This approach is precise but complex, requiring managers to have a good understanding of the HR jargon. For each team member that they evaluate, managers must become familiar with the definition of the competency and descriptors at each level in order to select which one is suitable. If managers must evaluate seven to 10 competencies for each team member, which is often the case, they end up with a lot of paperwork to read.

As I find this approach difficult to apply in companies, I often use a unique definition of competency with associated behaviors, but without these descriptors at each proficiency level.

Thus, to evaluate competencies, managers use an expertise grid of four or five levels such as the one pictured below. People can directly apply the grid to the corresponding behaviors.

This approach is based on similar definitions of expertise levels to those of Benjamin Bloom's taxonomy of educational objectives.[8]

---

8 https://en.wikipedia.org/wiki/Benjamin_Bloom

Levels	Skills-based
5. Expert	Design system, manual, procedure Support other department/companies The go-to person in the organization
4. Specialist	Guide/train others Receive full delegation and autonomy from their supervisor or manager
3. Professional	Work alone most of the time, with little follow up of their work
2. Junior	Need close supervision, guidance, and reporting
1. Beginner	Might have some knowledge on theory but needs training to develop skills

Figure 3.2: Example of expertise levels grid

With many of these systems, we spend months writing suitable definitions of competencies and their proficiency levels, eventually using existing databases. In fact, the most difficult part is using the competencies to evaluate people at work. This step is often not given the importance it deserves. Companies hurry to write behaviors and descriptors of competencies, called a dictionary of competencies, and ask managers to implement the system without providing the necessary information and training on how to apply these definitions when they evaluate their team members.

The evaluation of competencies should be based on a set of proofs. But it can't be 100% scientific, like it could when evaluating the size of a chair or a car on the production line. Considering my engineering background, I wish it were the case! Often, companies want to implement a system that is too complicated.

The main purpose of evaluation is to generate discussions around the behavior of the team member being evaluated. Using it to justify salary increases or bonuses should be done carefully. That is why I recommend only doing so after several years of implementing the competency system for less sensitive issues like training, recruitment, or career development.

Then, people in the company have time to build a good understanding and alignment on the way to evaluate.

So, as a consultant, how do I implement a suitable competency system to support governments or companies?

In the past, I was inclined to use *the* model that I believed was suitable, which, of course, was often the French model. However, it sometimes ended up being too complicated for users. Indeed, it required them to change their initial approach, or the model did not fit with their organization's culture, in the same way that putting a lot of tantalizing Thai spices on French food does not always lead to a delicious meal.

Today, my approach is simple: *be flexible*! Find out which system is already used in the organization and what existing knowledge and references people already have.

If the organization already has an HR management system based on the British model, for example, then I recommend using that country's approach, along with their vocabulary and structure. I often try to simplify it, especially in the case of the evaluation method, by using an expertise-level grid (beginner, junior, professional, specialist, expert), if possible.

I have used this flexible approach to implement competency systems for various governments and companies:

- I applied the French model in a Vietnamese-French cooperation project to transfer five French competency-based vocational education programs: The two-year curriculum would ultimately train students in 20 to 30 key competencies. For example, the competency in the automotive maintenance curriculum of "measure, test, try a system, a subsystem, a vehicle component" was defined using three steps of work, 12 performance criteria and 11 kinds of resources.
- I used the British model for garment jobs in Asian countries: This involved writing an 80-page document describing 20-30 units of competencies (e.g., "prepare and conduct negotiation") with four to seven corresponding elements

and details of all the knowledge, skills, evidence, range, and resources needed to teach and assess them.

♦ I designed a competency assessment system in a Thai conglomerate using the American model: This involved having a list of eight core (e.g., "responsibility"), five managerial, and a hundred functional competencies with corresponding definitions and five levels of behaviors.

♦ I designed a classifications system based on small competencies (skills) to support workers' career paths in construction and manufacturing companies: Each job (e.g., painter) was defined with four or five main skills and corresponding criteria.

♦ I built a competency system with corresponding evaluation mixing 20 general competencies based on the Harvard Dictionary (e.g., "managing performance") and a list of 200 functional competencies corresponding to every function (e.g., sales, production, finance) for a manufacturing company, with a simple definition (e.g., "to compute, report, and pilot the tax obligations").

This variety of approaches of competency systems is summarized below:

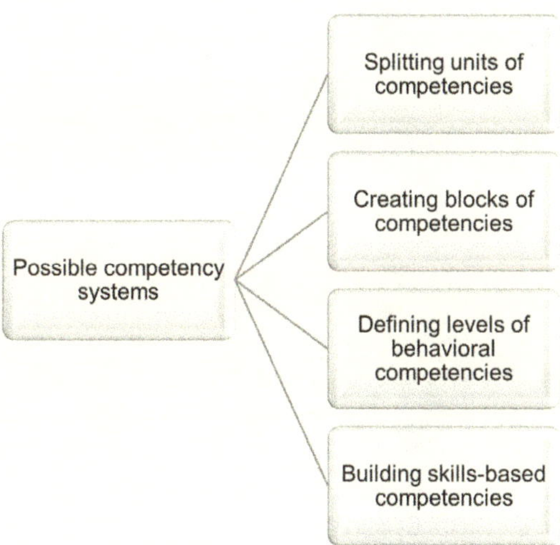

Figure 3.3. Examples of competency systems

Conclusion

So, as we can see, the world of competency systems is rather complex. There is not a "one size fits all" approach. Companies, organizations, and governments must tailor their approach in order to fit to their culture, context, and available resources for implementation.

Going back to the training in Thailand which I described at the beginning of the chapter, by asking participants to analyze various competency systems instead of transferring one unique model, I was encouraging them to develop two competencies that I try to use while implementing these systems and that are much needed in the 2023 world: *flexibility* and *analytical thinking*!

4. MY LIFELONG SELF-DEVELOPMENT

As you might have understood by now, the main topic of this book is people development.

It's all very well to talk about helping other people develop their skills, but why not lead by example and talk about how I develop *myself*?

If consultants like me don't develop their skill sets, their competencies, and themselves, they will not bring any value to customers and partners, who will end up not needing them anymore!

I would like to share with you the 10 methods I use to develop myself to bring (and keep bringing!) value to my customers and partners.

1. Training (participation in face-to-face group training)

Nowadays, everyone talks about online learning. As I mentioned in a previous chapter, I believe that a good face-to-face training session cannot be replaced with a Zoom video call. I have followed training in various countries (e.g., Thailand, France, and England), and they all were essential to strengthen my knowledge on topics such as the return on investment of training, coaching, competencies, e-learning, etc. These training sessions also provided opportunities to share experiences with other people.

While the possibilities are endless, I usually go on a training course when I have one of the following three needs:

- ♦ Implementing a future project (e.g., competency system)
- ♦ Developing a new expertise (e.g., measurement of return on investment, e-learning)
- ♦ Strengthening skills needed to implement my existing projects (e.g., coaching skills)

2. Online training

This form of learning has really developed since the COVID-19 pandemic. I prefer longer courses which run over several weeks with assignments between each session, accompanied by video content and participants sharing experiences. This is particularly the case with soft skills. For instance, I once did a training session on coaching skills which had all of the above, but there were still some weaknesses. I felt frustrated that there was not enough real practice (online) to motivate me. Having practical activities is especially important because, being online, we have more tendency to lose focus. Moreover, when the trainer is well known, as they were in this case, the organizer is likely to recruit many participants from all over the world, and this reduces the opportunities for interactions, simulations, and practice during the session.

3. Associations

I am a member of several professional associations focusing on business development, gaining experience, and knowledge exchange.

My favorite one is Toastmaster International,[9] which helps me develop public speaking and leadership skills. This association has groups all over the world and more than 10 in Bangkok alone.

9 https://www.toastmasters.org/

How many conferences, training sessions, or meetings have we attended where most people were sleeping, playing, talking, eating, basically doing anything except listening? This association helps me to make a seven-minute speech and keep the attention of the audience, whether it is in front of two or 2,000 people, and whether the purpose is to train, to share a story, or to summarize a 200-page HRD book.

Through this association, I get to practice preparing and presenting speeches, give feedback on others' speeches, and learn to strip out all those unnecessary words that we say to fill in the gaps (um, ah, so, well). In addition to developing my public speaking skills, the variety of situations and roles (speech giver, evaluator, master of ceremony) enable me, and others, to strengthen leadership skills.

I can only recommend joining a similar association as it has provided a safe space for personal improvement outside of my company. In this association, people of all different ages and nationalities help each other to reach similar goals.

4. Seminars and webinars

Participation in seminars (physical presence) and webinars (online) bring me new perspectives, not so much new skills.

I go to specialized ones, such as the annual HR Tech Seminar in Bangkok, as well as more general ones, like from the Association for Talent Development (ATD), either in person (e.g., in Singapore for the Asian perspectives) or online.

For instance, once, I registered for the ATD online seminar. I was impressed by its quality:

- Sessions were very focused.
- Some speakers presented high-quality videos and demonstrations of learning situations.
- Interaction was encouraged through quizzes, polls, and

> sharing ideas on a chat. We could directly plan online
> meetings with the people we wanted to connect with.
> ♦ Participants were able to access all presentation materials
> within one month after the seminar.

ATD did as much as they could to make the experience memorable within the limitations of the online setting. But towards the end, my concentration still faltered because it was online. I ended up doing what we shouldn't do: keeping only one eye on the online presentation while doing other activities at the same time, like answering emails.

5. Being a trainer

As the researcher William Glasser said, we remember 90% of the information we present or train others on.

Being a trainer has been a great way to reinforce my skills on topics as varied as coaching, feedback, cross-culture, competency systems, people development, management, etc. As a trainer, I now know these subjects better because:

- ♦ I need to remember the knowledge in order to present it.
- ♦ I continuously look for new training content that could bring value to my trainees.
- ♦ I get tips, ideas, and learn about participants' experiences.
- ♦ I am challenged by participants' comments, which force my brain to structure my knowledge better.

6. Project-based reading

Let's be real. Consultants rarely know everything they need to, which makes continual learning essential. When I read books to improve my knowledge, I follow four steps:

1. Identify the knowledge gap.
2. Select and read the relevant book.
3. Write down key points on four to seven pages: We remember more by writing on paper than by typing on a keyboard!
4. Integrate that key information into the project.

This is a very convenient method these days. It used to take me two or three weeks to get books from the US but now, with my Kindle, I can have them in two minutes.

7. Mentors and work partners or customers

Over the past 35 years, I have had French mentors who helped me build my confidence by sharing their experience (and becoming friends!). In addition, I have had many memorable working experiences with partners on international projects, based on common respect and knowledge sharing. For example:

♦   Several French colleagues shared with me their vision of learning through embracing emotions, participation of learners, group dynamics, and active listening.

♦   A Thai partner taught me that "in developing countries, we know what to do to improve education because we have been trained and we read books, but our difficulty lies in how to do it and how to implement it to adapt to our local context." This formed the basis of my company's vision.

♦   A Vietnamese customer taught me the value of patience and tenacity during lengthy discussions to find consensus on the implementation of our project.

♦   A Lao customer impressed me with her vision, knowledge, the multiple languages she spoke, as well as her participative approach when managing her team.

- ◆ Experts from international organizations, like one Australian team leader who taught me the importance of reviewing data collection before planning new projects; an American coordinator pushing me to analyze more deeply in my report; and the Finnish team leader who showed me how to lead with simplicity and care.
- ◆ And so many others …

8. E-learning and massive open online courses (MOOCs)

Being online allows us to learn quickly and whenever we want. However, the PowerPoint-based MOOCs I had done lacked interaction. I need to be pushed or to have a precise objective otherwise I am easily distracted. Maybe if I selected MOOCs with an exam at the end, I would have followed them more carefully.

That being said, I have enjoyed well-designed e-learning modules from Cegos and Harvard, as these integrated various learning modalities. There were interactive games, question-and-answer sessions, and quizzes. Knowledge was passed on through articles, slides, videos, and PDF documents that I could download. I was motivated by action plans and self-reflection questions. But, in the end, the most important thing is that I applied some of this knowledge to my projects.

9. Podcasts

They are all over the internet.

My favorite podcast about leadership is *Coaching for Leaders*[10]. I like it because: 1) The topics are relevant; 2) Speakers are experts; 3) Content is practical and applicable; 4) Most of the time, participants make sure to speak slowly and the sound quality is good. This point is particularly important for a non-native English speaker like me who has trouble understanding

---

10 http://coachingforleaders.com

certain British accents, such as Irish or Scottish (which is a pity because I've found the people from these countries are very nice!). In addition, the moderator-owner of the podcast is friendly, humble, and asks insightful questions. He mainly invites consultants as they are used to passing on knowledge, speaking slowly and clearly, providing precise tips and lessons learnt, not to mention the fact that they can share diverse experiences.

The podcast *The Look and Sound of Leadership*[11] explains how coaching can be used for people development and to share valuable guidelines and tools supporting communication in the workplace.

I also like to check out the Cedefop website, the reference for vocational training systems in Europe.

10. Social networks

Until 2020, I rarely used social media.

However, in January 2021, I started a project that changed that: I wrote two LinkedIn articles per month reviewing my 33 years of HRD experience.

This project was successful from both a quantitative point of view (I grew my network from 290 to 550 connections within a year) and qualitative (by engaging in discussions and reconnecting with people I had not talked to for many years).

Nowadays, I react or write comments as well as posts whenever I read something that could be valuable for my network. But I sometimes feel overwhelmed by this world of information: the inspiring leadership quotes, the personal stories, the product promotion. I try to be selective and focus on topics that support my professional development.

That being said, as I am already busy implementing all the learning and development methods we discussed in previous chapters, I have very little time left, which puts me among the very few people in Thailand who don't have a Facebook account.

---

11 https://essentialcomm.com/podcast

Here they are, the 10 ways to develop my knowledge and skills.

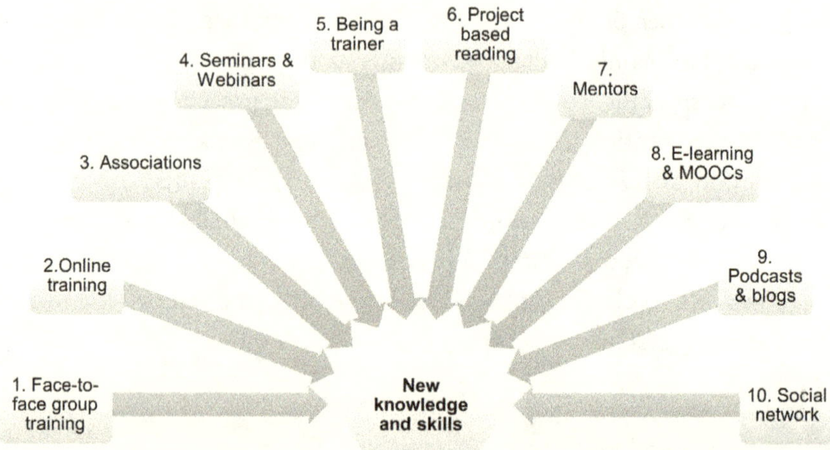

Figure 4.1: Ten ways to develop my knowledge and skills

Conclusion

The longer I work, the more people ask me when I am going to retire. This question is probably relevant, considering I am now into my 60s. But I continue to love my job, even after all these years, so I am not planning to retire early. If I want to bring value to the HRD system of partners and customers, I need to lead by example and continue developing myself by using these 10 ways to learn: This is what we call "lifelong learning"!

5. LEADERS ARE IMPORTANT: BUT HOW TO DEVELOP THEM?

In this chapter, I explain how I apply my nine concepts shared in the first chapter to leadership development programs. Why? Because they are one of the most challenging kinds of training programs to implement successfully.

More than 30 years ago, I was recruited as an HRD consultant in one of the largest French training companies. The branch where I was based, in Lyon, was unique in that the team of consultants shared a common vision of a learner-centered pedagogy. Their fundamental goal was to see people growing personally and professionally. They promoted experiential learning, active listening, participative (trainee-trainer relations), and interactive (trainees-trainees' relations) pedagogy. They had a lot of experience – the average age in this organization was 48!

I will always be grateful to them. The seven years I spent working with them helped shape my vision of learning for the rest of my career.

After spending my two first years under their mentorship, I was assigned the responsibility to plan, organize, follow up, and monitor one of the flagship management development programs. At that time, "leadership" was not the magic word that it is now.

The program included 30 days spread over 14 months, with three training days per month using a learner-centered approach. There were assignments between each session as well as regular debriefing meetings between each trainee manager and their superiors to follow up on their behavior changes. This program was well known among our customers; they sent their managers to follow the course every year. I really enjoyed managing it.

Many years later, in Thailand, I was reminded of this experience when I encountered a drastically different approach. The HR manager of one of the largest Thai industrial conglomerates told me about an issue they were facing, "Each year, we organize a management development program for 30 managers where we invite professors from a famous US university. They learn over the course of one full month, with many business cases, but we do not see clear behavior changes when our managers go back to work."

My immediate thought was, how can he expect a change of management vision and practices in such a short time? The program is packed, too packed, and therefore does not provide the necessary time for maturation, integration, nor adaptation to everyday reality.

I told him, "You are mixing two approaches: education and training. Education requires time for the brain to process new behaviors, skills, and visions being learnt. This is what I found during my master's degree in vocational training project management. Training is about developing identified skills quickly."

With that in mind, I helped him redesign the program using a project-based approach of training modules distributed over several months. This new program is still in use today.

For the past five years, I have implemented two kinds of leadership development programs.

Both are based on the well-known **70-20-10 model**, which stipulates that learning brings behavior change at work if it is based on 10% formal learning, 70% application at work of this formal learning, and 20% receiving feedback on this practice at work. These numbers are not literal but a guideline, and they show the importance of implementing the learning at work.

The overall process can be symbolized like this:

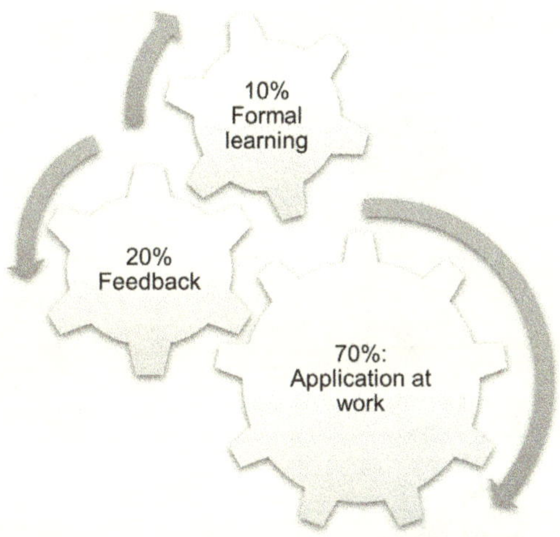

Figure 5.1: The 70-20-10 people development model

The first kind of leadership development program that I implemented comprehensively integrates the three elements of the 70-20-10 model:

- Five days of training distributed over several months using a learner-centered method including the following each day
    - 30-40 slides on theory and management tools but not more
    - No lecture longer than 20 minutes
    - Various interactive activities
    - At the beginning of each module, a one-hour session to review the application of the learning of the previous module at work
    - During the module, regular self-reflection and writing of action plans
- E-learning modules
- Quizzes sent by HR to all participants between each session to strengthen the learning process
- Action learning sessions to solve management problems in groups

♦ Individual coaching sessions implemented by the trainer with each participant.

Timeframe / Activity	Month 1		Month 2		Month 3		...
Training modules		Module 1: Leadership		Module 2: Change		Module 3:	
Learning reinforcement		Online quiz on module 1		Online quiz on module 2			Online quiz on module 4
E-learning modules	2h: Be a leader		2h: Change		2h: Giving feedback		
Meeting with direct supervisor	1h: individual meeting: infor-mation		1h: Follow up action plan		1h: Follow up action plan		1h: Evaluation ofchanges
Coaching with trainer	1h: Plan learning						1h: Evaluate learning and changes
Action learning			3h: Problem-solving				

Figure 5.2: Example of 70-20-10 model for a leadership development program

The second kind of leadership development program is much more individualized and very focused. It is often called an individual development plan (IDP). The learner identifies one skill to develop, such as giving feedback, asking questions, or delegating, and the 70-20-10 approach is applied within a precise time frame (e.g., three months):

♦ 10%: Formal learning comes from reading a book, listening to a podcast, e-learning.

♦ 70%: The application of this learning is executed in precise, identified situations at work.

♦ 20%: The learner receives feedback by sharing successes and difficulties during the implementation of the key learning at work. This feedback is provided by an accountability partner who can be their manager, a colleague, a friend, or an expert. Regularity is essential.

This IDP can be represented as follows.

<table>
<tr><td>Competency to develop: Delegation</td></tr>
<tr><td>Time frame: January 2024-April 2024</td></tr>
<tr><td>

Experiential learning (70%):
1. List the topics I need to delegate (e.g., new process) and the purpose of this delegation (impacts for both team and myself)
2. Schedule the delegation of topics
3. Decide who I will delegate those topics to; communicate it
4. Identify skills gaps using skills matrix
5. Define the individual development plan using the skills matrix
6. Implement and monitor (one-to-one) the delegation plan following the schedule
7. Present the results of the delegation: who has which competency?

</td></tr>
<tr><td>

Social learning; receiving feedback from others (20%):
Every two weeks, I will have a one-to-one meeting with Mrs. A. She has a lot of experience delegating tasks. She will provide feedback and advice on my delegation method.

</td></tr>
<tr><td>

Formal learning (10%):
I will follow the two e-learning modules, delegation steps and situational management, and present the key points to Mrs. A. with a five-slide summary for each e-learning.

</td></tr>
</table>

Figure 5.3: Example of 70-20-10 individual development plan

The key to success with the 70-20-10 model is how the 70% is implemented and connected to the 10% (formal learning). Learning at work (70%) is challenging because people are under pressure to deliver results, so they do not take time to learn and reflect on what they have been taught. When I implement this system with managers in companies, I always tell them that this learning at work (70%) is not "doing the day job" as it requires applying the new knowledge gained during formal learning (10%) and from the feedback received (20%).

With the development of online self-learning (e-learning, MOOC, etc.) since COVID-19, this individualized 70-20-10 model is proving to be especially suitable. It can reduce the use of traditional formal training significantly, which cuts training costs (and that always makes my customers happy!). However, in the case of learning soft skills, I believe that a good trainer will always have more impact than a good e-learning course. The human aspect is still crucial!

In 2022, a company contacted me because they wanted someone to implement a leadership development program in several countries, including Thailand. They sent me the program, but I declined because I didn't believe it would bring significant behavior change. Why? Because it was based on a series of modules without a clear mechanism to connect them to everyday work. I was expecting to implement the 70-20-10 process described above.

Many learning modalities within this 70-20-10 model are possible. Personally, I split them into the following five categories.

Print and mass media-based learning	Reading papers, e-books, reports, studies, journals, etc.
Group-based learning	Workshops, seminars, training, online training (one trainer teaching several people at the same time), online community-based learning
Work-based learning	Assignment or implementation of a new project, such as repairing/installing a machine or a process, new management organization, software, etc.
One-on-one-based learning	Coaching by an external expert, mentoring by an older and more experienced teacher or manager
Internet-based learning	Webinars, videoconferencing (usually small lectures of 30 to 60 minutes with one or several lecturers), MOOCs, e-learning or microlearning, podcasts, videos, games

Figure 5.4: Five learning modalities

The World Bank has produced a very comprehensive practical guide describing "The Art of Knowledge Exchange"[12] including 10 instruments which support short-term, medium-term, and long-term learner engagement as well as 25 kinds of activities split into four categories (presentation, discussion, experimental, analytical).

However, this efficient blended learning model is also being disrupted.

At the end of 2021, a customer contacted me and asked, "Arnauld, I have a 30-page manual on negotiation and the corresponding PowerPoint presentation. My customers are all over the world so I can't do face-to-face training. I have a good mobile learning application. Can you transfer this manual to mobile learning?"

Doubtful but curious, I followed a course on mobile instructional design and created a microlearning program which mixed seven kinds of open and closed questions or assignments with small bits of learning content. Each activity lasted no more than five minutes. Participants could access it anytime and anywhere. It was easier to prepare than I thought it would be. I will explain the details of this approach in another chapter.

I enjoyed this experience as it showed me that I can apply some of my nine principles in a completely different approach and still be part of the digital transformation!

All in all, even if this new model of leadership development program using microlearning is not perfect, its efficiency and simplicity sparked questions in my mind: Could, and will, the leadership development programs based on the 70-20-10 model and all corresponding learning modalities (training, e-learning, coaching, etc.) be replaced by *simple but efficient micro-learning programs on smartphones?*

Conclusion

The 70-20-10 development model enables the application of the majority of the nine learning principles mentioned in the first chapter, for

---

12 The World Bank (2017). The Art of Knowledge Exchange.

the development of all staff but especially for the soft skills required by team leaders.

I believe, and I am not the only one, that the integration of formal learning, getting feedback, and application at work produces a real behavioral change and sustainable skills development.

The efficiency of this approach can be supported by various learning modalities such as print and mass media-based learning, group-based learning, work-based learning, one-on-one-based learning, and internet-based learning.

HR managers and decision-makers can select the most appropriate method depending on the learner background, expected outcomes, environment, and available resources.

And it is expected that this scope of learning possibilities will be definitively explored in the future thanks to the evolution of technologies.

6. DISRUPTION IN THE LEARNING SYSTEMS: HOW TO AVOID BEING A DINOSAUR

In May 2018, I went to an HR tech seminar in Bangkok on the topic of new technology applications in HR management and development. Experts made presentations on how learning and development are being disrupted by internet-based learning. Suppliers demonstrated various innovative solutions. I had walked into this seminar with confidence built by years of experience. At the end of the day, I walked out humbled, with one horrifying question stuck in my head: *Am I already a dinosaur?*

That seminar marked the beginning of my journey into the world of internet-based learning modalities and how they can increase efficiency of learning and development.

Let's review these modalities. Overall, they can be divided into two approaches: asynchronous and synchronous.

1. **Synchronous approach:** The activity happens at a fixed time with a facilitator or trainer.

    1.1. I have adapted some of my face-to-face training to be *online,* mainly due to the COVID-19 pandemic. I usually like to plan short sessions with a small number of participants and include different interactions. In a later chapter, I will discuss how to make these kinds of interventions successful, in my experience.

1.2. *Webinars and online seminars* that I have taken part in have usually lasted 30 minutes to two hours. One or several lecturers present their PowerPoint, then there's a question-and-answer session followed by small questionnaires or quizzes. As interesting as they might be, it is only one-way communication, so I lose my concentration and, suddenly, I will find myself reviewing my emails while listening "from one ear only," as the French say.

At the end of 2021, I had the opportunity to organize a seminar with a different approach. The purpose was to present a study that I coordinated for an international organization on the implementation of the learner-centered teaching method in vocational education in six countries in the Asia-Pacific region. For the final workshop, the six national consultants involved in the project had to share their results individually. Instead of having them spend 30 minutes each presenting their results, we implemented a flipped workshop. I provided a precise PowerPoint template of 12 slides to each expert and had them transpose their reports onto this template and send them to their colleagues from the five other countries and other participants in the workshop. Each expert had to read their colleagues' PowerPoints and prepare five questions each. There was no actual presentation of the results but only direct questions and answers. It was challenging to manage the time and scope of the questions, but all participants expressed satisfaction with the level of interaction (and I got to use a "learner-centered" approach on this learner-centered project!).

2. Asynchronous approach: There is no fixed time, no trainer, and we can learn whenever we want.

2.1. *E-learning* modules were the first significant breakthrough in internet-based learning. They were created for computers, thus not exactly suitable for use on smartphones due to the kind of content and exercises proposed. E-learning modules that I have completed were structured with precise learning objectives. They ranged from 30 minutes to two hours and were composed of exercises, tests, videos, text, quizzes, open questions for reflection, and documents to download.

E-learning can be fun and interactive. It's important to remember: They are not PowerPoint presentations. I was once asked to work on a project for a company producing and selling mechanical parts for the construction industry. This company had 26 so-called "e-learning" modules of 30 minutes to two hours each, presenting products and machines sold by the company. It was basically a series of PowerPoint presentations read by their engineers. There was very little interaction except a short quiz at the end. As a result, the quality was inconsistent: some spoke in a monotonous tone, others too fast or too slow, and the presentations contained grammatical errors, to name just a few issues. The HR manager was not happy with the level of attendance of these modules considering that it was essential staff knew the content. A change was definitely needed.

We completely restructured these modules by breaking down all presentations into small chunks of a few minutes and including short exercises and interactions. In some sessions, we planned more than 20 activity changes within the one-hour session!

The plan looked a bit like this:

Time	Topic	Activity	Detailed and learning aids
10'	Product features	Read	Four to five slides on basic principles of the machine
		Do	Quiz
10'	Technical performance	Watch	Video on the performance
		Do	Quiz

25′	Process	Read	Three slides on processes
		Write	The differences of three processes
		Read	Two slides on quality control
		Watch	Video on traceability of product certificate
		Do	Matching game

Figure 6.1: Example of e-learning plan

Together with the HR specialist of the company, we managed to create more than 30 modules which are now being used for staff training, especially for newcomers. It was satisfying to see the managers who created the initial PowerPoints accept this change and witness the increased attendance.

2.2. Hundreds of thousands of *MOOCs* are now available, thanks to all the experts, training organizations, and universities which give us access to great content. It is mainly one-way communication. For example, I did a 30-hour-long MOOC on learning systems which was essentially a Power-Point presentation with exercises and quizzes.

2.3. *Online podcasts and videos* are available on every topic you could imagine. Most of the ones I know or follow last a maximum of one hour. I can listen to experts, specialists, and gurus. There is no interaction; it's totally up to me and my motivation as to how I apply any learning.

2.4. *Smartphone applications:* They can be used in different ways, as I explain below.

Smartphones apps for learning

The use of smartphone apps for learning is supported by neuroscientific research: Learning is more likely to "stick" if it's split into small parts and if it's spaced, repeated, challenging, and motivating (see Chapter 1).

I already knew some basics through discussions with my two children. I noticed that they were using a well-known app to learn languages, which I'm sure you've heard of: Duolingo. Intrigued, I questioned them about it. They would never say it out loud because they wouldn't want to hurt my feelings, but I could feel it in the way they were explaining the concept to me: In the world of learning methods, I was becoming a dinosaur.

So, after my participation in the HR tech seminar mentioned at the beginning of this chapter, I typed "smartphones for learning" into Google. I was overwhelmed, to say the least!

I read articles, studies, blogs; I spent hours talking to smartphone app providers in the US, Switzerland, Thailand, and Singapore; and I compared the kinds of questions used, analytics, designs, and references of these various apps. I also followed some online training on mobile instructional design.

It took me some time, but I finally clarified the three ways to use smartphone apps for learning and development. And most importantly, I experimented with them.

1. Microlearning

Instead of face-to-face training, we receive chunks of knowledge on our phone over a couple of weeks in a highly interactive process. I implemented this system for a client who asked me to transfer a three-day, face-to-face training course on negotiation to a mobile application. I prepared a micro-learning program of around four hours based on more than 100 activity changes: reading a text, playing a matching game, doing a quiz, watching a video, reflecting on learning, choosing pictures, reading a powerful quote. Each activity lasted a few minutes. It was highly interactive and took me only about two days to complete the transfer.

2. Learning reinforcement

In this case, the smartphone app is used to strengthen knowledge after it has been learnt in a traditional face-to-face session. I have used this method in leadership development programs on topics such as delegation or coaching. After each session and over the following three weeks, participants received small quizzes to review the knowledge they had learned. There was a competitive element in the process and a final reward was given to the person who got the highest score. I enjoyed this project a lot; it definitely made learning efficient and fun.

3. Training or behavior reinforcement

The difference here to above is that learners are asked questions to validate how much of the new knowledge they have been able to apply at work. For example, "How many times did you apply the feedback techniques in the past week?"

The most interesting application of this way of learning is Mindmarker,[13] created by a former Dutch judo champion. He transferred a method he used to strengthen his judo behaviors and gestures to the world of learning and development.

I implemented this application to support behavior change after a one-day training session on how to give feedback. Participants received six kinds of messages two or three times per week, with a mix of questions to raise awareness, transfer or review knowledge, and encourage the learner to apply the new learning at work, such as, "How much feedback did you give?" "How difficult was it?" "How are you planning to give feedback?" "What methods do you want to use?"

Here is an extract of the training (or behavior) reinforcement plan:

Time	Type of messages	Topic
Week 1, Day 1, 1.00 PM	Evaluation	Feedback introduction
Week 1, Day 1, 1.00 PM	Pitfall	Purpose of giving corrective feedback
Week 1, Day 3, 11.00 AM	Self-reflection	Reminder of corrective feedback

---

13 https://mindmarker.com/

Week 1, Day 4, 1.00 PM	Measure behavior change	Confidence in giving corrective feedback
Week 1, Day 5, 9.00 AM	Measure behavior change	Frequency in giving corrective feedback following a specific process
Week 2, Day 2, 11.00 AM	Measure knowledge	Most important components when giving corrective feedback
Week 2, Day 3, 11.00 AM	Measure knowledge	Feedback process
.....	...	
.....	...	
Week 5, Day 1, 1.00 PM	Measure behavior change	Confidence in giving corrective feedback
Week 5, Day 5, 9.00 AM	Measure behavior change	Frequency in giving corrective feedback following a specific process

Figure 6.2: Example of training reinforcement plan

I found this approach especially suitable for the development of soft skills and leadership skills that require a difficult change of habits and behaviors. Indeed, as highlighted by one of the most recognized coaches, Marshall Goldsmith, sustainable behavior changes require triggers and reminders.[14]

In addition, a precise data analytics system can be used to dissect the participants' answers.

These three ways of using smartphone applications have different purposes and modalities. As HRD specialists, we can choose the one that

---

14 Goldsmith, M. (2015) Triggers: Creating Behavior That Lasts – Becoming the Person You Want to Be. Currency

is suitable for our learning and development program and its expected learning outcomes.

But this new way of learning is also being disrupted. As I explained in the first chapter, the HRD field is changing.

This was made obvious to me in 2022, when I went to a seminar on learning and development. There, I discovered the power and the impact of *artificial intelligence (AI)* on learning, especially through these three approaches:

♦ Serious games and gamification: Around 20 years ago, a lot of people were addicted to computer games such as The Sims or Age of Empire. These strategy games are now used for learning and development. Back in the 1980s, I was in charge of a 30-day training program for managers. We started the program with a three-day "business game" based on several teams acting as companies competing against each other. Back then, we had to use pretty basic materials (papers, cards, tokens, etc.); looking back, it almost seems prehistoric. Today, the same concept of gamification of situations at work applies, but technology has advanced and the simulations of business situations are far more sophisticated, helping participants absorb new skills and knowledge.

♦ The metaverse: I am really not an expert on this, so it might be more helpful to quote a leading American resource on learning and development, Training Industry. In in one of their articles, they present this new concept and the opportunities it brings: "The metaverse opens the door to new possibilities for innovative ways to leverage digital learning solutions within a greater ecosystem ... early adoption of augmented and virtual reality (AR and VR) for onboarding and training allows learners to gain hands-on job experience in a remote, risk-free environment, and it enables people to problem solve more effectively in break-fix scenarios, which ultimately improves customer experiences." [15]

---

15 https://trainingindustry.com/articles/learning-technologies/
training-in-another-dimension-how-the-metaverse-will-impact-ld/

After gathering information from different sources, I have built a better understanding of why and how more and more companies are using the metaverse. This is notably the case for the process of onboarding, where new staff get to know their companies and colleagues by using special AR or VR goggles explaining everything that they need to know to support a quick integration.

♦ Artificial Intelligence Teaching Assistance (AITA)[16] builds groups of learners with similar profiles, suggests learning methods, and updates the data analytics of the learner. In 2023, the launch of the ChatGPT website generated a worldwide reaction on how it could be used to support learning and development. We are now just at the beginning of this learning adventure. Like everybody, I have started to use it to support my interventions and look forward to the disruption in the learning ecosystem that it will generate in the future.

I summarize all these learning approaches as follows:

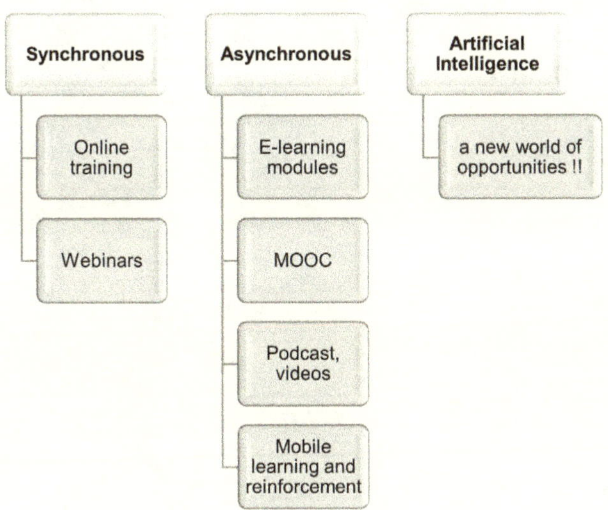

Figure 6.3: Internet-based learning approaches

---

16 Luckin, R. & Holmes, W. (2016) Intelligence Unleashed: An Argument for AI in Education. Pearson

Conclusion

The use of the internet, as summarized above, enables a variety of applications with synchronous or asynchronous approaches. This chapter reinforces the previous one on leadership development programs where I mentioned that we can now have access to a variety of learning modalities.

If I want to bring value to my customers and partners, I need to continue learning about all these internet-based applications. Plus, I will not look like a dinosaur in front of my children!

7. FROM OFFLINE TO ONLINE TRAINING: HEADACHES AND MEDICINES

In 2020, I got a call from an HR manager of a large Thai bank of 30,000 employees. I had already worked with the bank on several projects measuring the return on investment of their training programs, so I knew it quite well. I also was aware that, like many companies, it was concerned by cost. That day, on the phone, my correspondent told me that her CEO wanted to transfer hundreds of training courses online.

Technically, that wasn't a bad choice. If the CEO was looking at training as, above all, a cost, then of course, this decision makes sense. In theory, everybody is winning:

- The finance manager is happy because they spend less on transportation and hotels, and they can negotiate with trainers to reduce fees.
- HR managers have less logistical work and can invite more people to attend the training (which is good for the yearly training statistics).
- Participants don't lose time travelling to training.

But if the CEO considers training as an investment and expects his staff to change behaviors after the course, with a positive impact on the business, then the company runs the risk of losing out if this transfer is not done well.

In 2020, when the COVID-19 pandemic broke out, like many of my trainer colleagues, I had to transfer my traditional face-to-face training online. It was, for me, and for hundreds of thousands of trainers around the world, a culture shock.

In order to strengthen my skills in this area, I attended some online training in June 2020. Considering the topic was "how to do online training," I was expecting a good model. It was organized by a well-known French training institute and sounded very promising. In the end, it turned out to be extremely disappointing. It succeeded in one aspect: It showed me all the ways in which you could run a bad online training course!

At the end, I had the opportunity to evaluate the course. I wrote a list of 12 points for improvement. These included:

♦ Confusion of objectives between the ability to conduct online training and the ability to use software and applications.

♦ No introduction of the participants at the beginning of the session, even though strengthening relations among the group is even more important in the context of online training.

♦ No content synthesis.

♦ No presentation after small groups activities to add value to the knowledge of the group and participants.

♦ Asking participants to give feedback on other participants without group dynamics management.

♦ Long lectures and not enough use of participants' previous experience.

Of course, I understand that most of the mistakes were not specific to online training and could have also been made face-to-face. However, I felt them even more during this online session.

Since then, I have had the opportunity to implement many online training sessions and experienced many problems. No doubt you have also come across many of these issues before.

They include:

- The internet connection is not good: sound is lost or the video freezes.
- The trainee's video does not work (although I never know if they are telling the truth or not).
- The trainees don't have access to a computer and use their smartphone: You can imagine the difference between a PowerPoint presentation or a PDF file downloaded on a smartphone compared to a laptop.
- There is too much background noise and the trainees have to turn off their microphone most of the time. I have heard all kinds of sounds: piano music, street traffic, children crying, dogs barking, crowing roosters, etc.
- I can't see participants' faces because they don't have good lighting, or an optimal setting or position.
- Trainees don't look me in the eyes because their camera is at the top of their screen or they use a second screen.
- I can't see what they really write when I give them the assignment.
- I can't walk towards less attentive or distracted trainees and engage with them.
- When I look at the trainees' eyes, I can see that they are doing something else, such as reading their emails, and therefore not really listening to me or to the other trainees.
- Conversations become stilted as we wait for people to turn their microphones back on, or if the connections drops out.
- They are not focused due to personal constraints at home (for example, having to take care of their children).

And, perhaps the most important aspect: I just can't feel their presence in the same way I would in face-to-face training. You probably know the 93/7 rule that 93% of communication occurs through nonverbal behavior and tone, while only 7% is through words.

Considering Ebbinghaus' research, which demonstrated that people forget 80% of the content of the training three days after the session, imagine what happens if we add the problems listed above.

So, then, how do I **manage my training online**?

First of all, I try to use *half-day sessions*, if possible in the morning when most participants will be more alert and active.

I always *stand* rather than sit in front of the screen so that I act more like how I would in a training room. I feel more energized standing than I do sitting in front of the screen. I use my hands more and my body language is more dynamic.

My wife bought me a special *light* for video calls. It turned out to be one of her best buys during the COVID-19 period. The light is in front of me, next to my screen and camera, and I can regulate its power and color tone.

I use *headphones* to reduce external noise so my trainees don't hear my neighbor's dog barking (once, a client actually asked me if I had a dog in my office). The sound I hear is clear and I increase my chances of having my speech being understood clearly, which is particularly helpful when I speak a foreign language like English or Thai.

I am *constantly interacting* with the participants. Research says that attention decreases sharply after 20 minutes during a face-to-face presentation, and this goes down to eight minutes in front of a screen. I'm inclined to believe that it's even less. Therefore, I make sure that I present a maximum of three to five slides in a row before doing an exercise, and I often make these interactive. For example, instead of presenting, I ask questions like, "What do you understand about this slide?"

I split participants into virtual *breakout rooms* to enable small groups activities. I follow up constantly with each group, which means that I enter their breakout room several times to check in because they often misunderstand the assignment given during the plenary session. I found that if the assignment takes around 15 to 20 minutes, there should be no more than five small groups to enable a good follow up with each one.

I write all the individual or group assignments very precisely on a *slide* with blanks that the participants will have to fill in.

What I need to improve is the use of available *applications* supporting learning activities during the online session. There are hundreds of them. How to choose? Jane Hart created a well-known and very useful compilation of what's available called, "The Top 10 (Digital) Tools for Learning."[17]

These are some of the key elements that I try to use, but there are many other ways to enable efficient online training. That includes asking funny questions in the chat, playing games to build a positive atmosphere, adding movement and body stretches (trainees often have to sit for long hours), asking participants to place objects in front of the camera or to react with emojis, polls, a gesture, etc., incorporating moments away from the screen (writing with pen and paper, for example), or using music.[18]

However, there's no point having the best tools if they are not integrated into a good learning process. I pay a lot of attention to pedagogy to ensure it supports efficient learning.

Experience has shown me that it takes longer to do the same training online than in a physical setting. Activities designed for use offline also need to be adapted to the online context.

Once, a client asked me to transfer a one-day training course for 15 people online. I told him that I would prefer to have a maximum of 12 people per group and split the one-day session into two half days, both in the morning when people tend to concentrate better. In addition, the second session allowed us to review the knowledge learnt during the first session (the importance of repetition, as explained in my nine principles in Chapter 1).

In a similar situation, in early 2019, I signed a contract to implement several two-day training sessions for multiple groups of trainers. Due to the COVID-19 crisis, I changed the process to several half-day online coaching and training sessions with teams of four or five trainers focusing on the essential key messages – the "need to know" – of training and removing all unnecessary content – the "nice to know." After these online sessions, we were able to plan a one-day physical workshop on facilitation skills.

---

17 https://www.toptools4learning.com/
18 https://www.trainers-toolbox.com/mastering-online-training-my-top-10-tips/

By adapting the session when transferring it online, rather than just leaving it as is, it continues to be productive. Flexibility is the key word here.

I sum up below the way I adapt to online training with eight key tips:

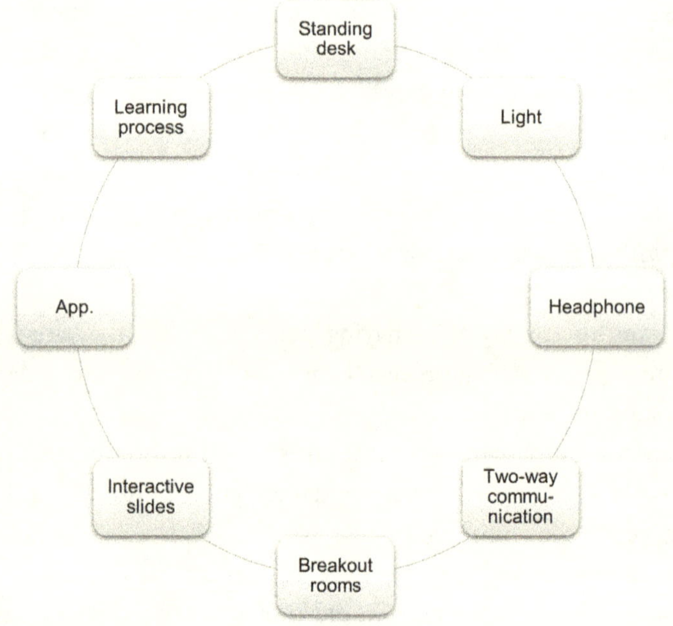

Figure 7.1: Eight tips to turn offline training into online training

Conclusion

The digitalization trend, accelerated by the COVID-19 pandemic, has supported the development of new behaviors. People are now used to working and learning in any place. However, the future should not be transferring all training programs online, as the CEO mentioned at the beginning of the chapter wanted to do. Instead, I am happy to move towards blended learning, mixing online and offline approaches. I believe that this flexibility of training approaches will be essential to adapt to the new behaviors of learners.

PART 2:

HOW TO IMPLEMENT HRD SYSTEMS?

8. TRANSFERRING NEW HRD SYSTEMS BUT MAKING THEM SUSTAINABLE

A couple of years ago, I was having lunch with the HR manager of a large electricity company in Thailand. He opened up to me about some issues he was having, "Arnauld, we have implemented 50 different systems in our company: KPI, competency, ISO 9000, TPM, ISO 14000, risk management, performance ... but none of them work as they should."

I couldn't believe it. How can none of these systems work? But then, I thought about it.

I implement HRD systems for companies and governments for a living. Once I have finished the assignment, its future is out of my hands. I often don't know if the system implemented will be sustainable, or if it will slowly be put aside, gathering dust in a filing cabinet or in neat folder on a computer which nobody opens.

Through years of practice, I have identified three key factors which help these HRD systems work and are sustainable.

1. Define what to transfer

Transferring a foreign model of HRD (e.g., vocational education curricula, teaching methods, quality systems, qualification standards) to another country is not easy. We need to translate or create manuals, methods, and procedures based on a (hopefully) successful system from another country. All this has to be integrated into the existing system and culture.

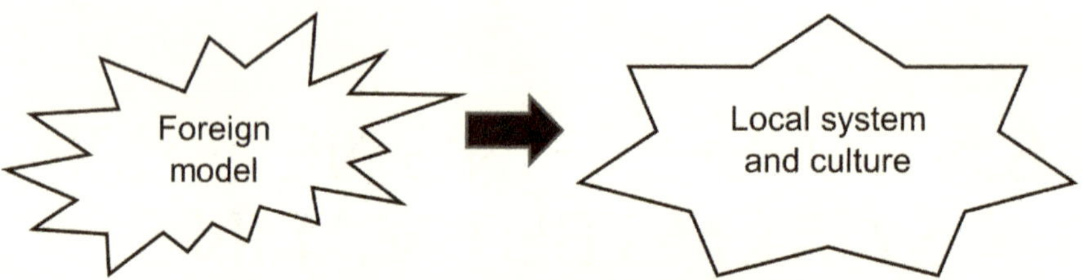

Figure 8.1: The challenge of integrating a foreign model into a local context

In the case of international cooperation projects, a developing country requests funding, a grant, or a loan from a development partner to improve their existing vocational education or skills development system. These development partners can be international organizations (ADB, World Bank, ILO, etc.) or countries with a more sophisticated HRD system (e.g., Germany, France, UK, Switzerland, etc.). The international partner proposes a new HRD system, as mentioned above, and, often, after some years, it becomes clear that this new system isn't sustainable, or only some of the methods and training packages have been applied.

The issue is that, often, the local partners, especially at policy or management levels, want to copy the new model and its components in its entirety without taking into account that their team at the operational level (teachers, managers, company staff) might not meet the conditions needed to apply it (motivation, time, management support, infrastructures, budget, knowledge).

For example, nowadays, more countries are interested in using the national qualification system (NQF) where corresponding skills are developed in training centers. In addition, assessment centers assess the people who have been trained and certifying bodies certify these training or assessment centers spread all over the country. All of these organizations need qualified people and operating budgets. This system, which depends on having well-funded training centers, might work in rich developed countries but not in countries with limited budgets and human resources.

Thus, what to do if we want to address this issue of transferring foreign models? I share one approach that we used in a project I led. We had to transfer to Thai institutes the French system of competency-based training with all its components: the creation process, how to write the programs, the training methods, the training materials, the evaluation methods, the procedures between institutes and companies, etc. Many of these elements were new for my Thai partners from institutes, companies, and ministries.

Over the course of this five-year project, I had to decide, with the local partners, which approach to choose for each of these components:

- Transfer everything without any adaptation, which means inform the partners then copy, translate, and train people.
- Simplify the components before transferring them.
- Not transfer some parts which I deem to be too complicated and not adaptable to the local culture.

In a way, I felt bad when I decided not to transfer some of our French system because it assumed that the local partners didn't have the potential to implement a more complex foreign education system.

Time is needed to adapt to new systems and technologies. I remember a French researcher telling a Thai professor in a university where I was working, "We will give you the results of 10 years of research, but I advise you to experiment as we did to fully understand the importance of these new results." Similarly, the president of a Thai university once told me that it might be better to cooperate with universities from less advanced countries because, as there was a lower technology gap between both universities, it was easier to integrate it into the practice of teachers and curricula.

This careful approach of always reflecting on what and what not to transfer was thrown into jeopardy when, in an international project, the representatives of the local ministry of labor instructed us to copy 100% of the French programs without any adjustment. Negotiating a 10%-20%

adjustment of program content to the local context took time. But, during this experience, I understood that the success of this kind of full program transfer also depends on the motivation and amount of work that the partner is willing to put in to applying the new knowledge.

The issues are the same when working with companies: what to transfer and what to simplify in my model of good practices for HRD systems? I need to identify what degree of complexity I should offer. To give an example, I once had to implement a management training program in Thailand which had been prepared in France with the purpose of being disseminated to factories all over the world. When I received the PowerPoint, I changed three aspects in order to adapt it to the Thai context:

1. I simplified the concepts, words, and sentences to avoid translation issues.
2. I integrated methods such as round table, questionnaires, and presentations to make Thai participants ask me questions or give comments because I knew that they would say very little if I just asked them "what questions do you have?" or "what are your comments?"
3. I adjusted the content of some modules to fit Thai culture, such as the one on giving feedback, because I knew that the French tendency to be frank would not be very popular with Thai trainees.

2. Finding the right partner

This component is connected to the first one. If I'm able to find the right local partner(s), then more of the new systems can be transferred and implemented.

A couple of years ago, I was strengthening the HR system of a construction company. Every year, there was a new project: certification systems, competencies, training, performance improvement, etc. My counterpart,

Mr. S., was an engineer at the company. Year after year, he developed his HR skills working with me.

One day, I told the company director that Mr. S. could take my place as leader of the HR project meetings. I knew I had found *the* person who would ensure the system continued after my departure. Thirteen years later, he is still there as HR manager, in charge of the systems we prepared together.

I always try to identify *the* person who will take ownership of my consulting assignment and who has the power in the organization, the motivation, the time, and the potential to make the new HR system sustainable.

To succeed in finding the right person, I believe there are four key criteria:

- Power in the organization in order to make the project move forward
- Enough technical background in the concerned area
- A supporting team (especially a number two, direct report, when the contact person has a high position)
- Available time

Overall, the quality of the relationship I have with this person is the main factor. It will enable us to solve, or not, any difficulties throughout the project. While I was leading Thai and international projects during the COVID-19 pandemic, I was frustrated that I couldn't connect informally with people (chit-chat outside meetings, meals together, etc.). When, finally, it was possible to go abroad and meet people in person, we got to know each other better and the atmosphere of online meetings that followed became more friendly.

But issues arise if this key person leaves the company or organization before the system is transferred and fully integrated.

In the case of development projects, the scale is larger. Thus, I try to identify the organization that could lead the project and, within it, a project manager.

Once, I had to implement a vocational education project in an Asian country, and I went directly to the vocational education department. There, I found the staff to be very busy, overwhelmed by the management of large projects supported by international organizations. I then went to visit other departments in the Ministry of Education. I identified the department which was responsible for the development of the quality assurance system for vocational education institutes and needed external, technical advice. We led the implementation with this team, and the busy vocational education department just participated in the project as they didn't have the time to do it themselves.

3. Supporting behavior change

A couple of years ago, I was team leader of a cooperation project where the goal was to implement French vocational programs in local vocational colleges. This project had three phases:

Phase 1: Two years to transfer the French program (content, training materials, methods etc.) including translation into English and the local language.
Phase 2: One year to train people (teachers, managers) on this new program.
Phase 3: Two years of individual support for the practical implementation in local colleges.

Projects that aim to transfer new systems either to a company or to a country often have only the first two phases: transferring knowledge and training the relevant people. In many cases, there would be little time for the third phase: assisting the implementation. The project team assumes that training is enough.

In my experience, a long third phase is essential to change habits, solve problems, and build autonomy among the users of the new system in order to guarantee its sustainability.

I use this approach even for small projects. For example, in Thailand, I regularly have a contract with a customer to help their new managers implement the company's performance management system. Eventually, I will create a short half-day workshop for them, but I will always stress the importance of the follow-up phase: three to five one-hour individual coaching sessions with each manager every three weeks to review the way they implement the system.

In 2022, I read a book called *The Human Element*[19] that helped me understand that there are various reasons why people don't accept change. We all know that making people change their habits and behaviors is difficult. The human mind is more negative than positive; for example, people remember negative feedback more than positive feedback. Thus, instead of spending time explaining all the advantages of the new system, we should identify the frictions and find ways to reduce them.

Based on this book and other change management theories, I identified several methods to reduce resistance to change grouped as follows:

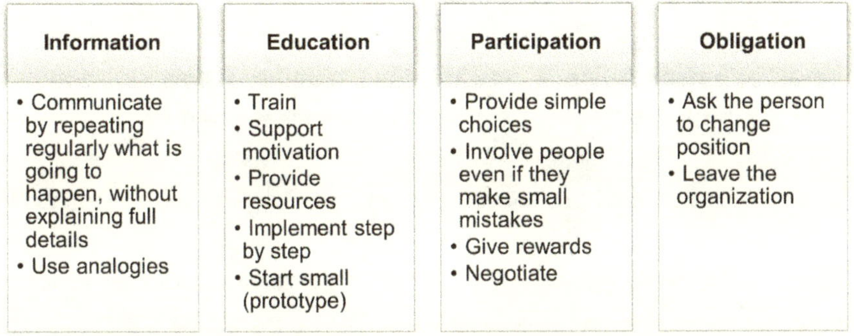

Information	Education	Participation	Obligation
• Communicate by repeating regularly what is going to happen, without explaining full details • Use analogies	• Train • Support motivation • Provide resources • Implement step by step • Start small (prototype)	• Provide simple choices • Involve people even if they make small mistakes • Give rewards • Negotiate	• Ask the person to change position • Leave the organization

Figure 8.2: Some methods to reduce resistance to change

And if people constantly reject the new system, giving them a long explanation is useless. I need to ask questions that I know they will say yes to, which in turn will allow them to reflect and slowly persuade themselves of the benefits.

---

19 Nordgren, L. & Schonthal, D. (2020) *The Human Element. Overcoming the Resistance That Awaits New Ideas.* Wiley

I try to implement these methods, but it is not always easy when I feel pressure to succeed in my projects. I can find myself in two awkward situations: 1) When I don't know a method or system well, I explain it more to show that I know it which, sometimes, causes confusion; and 2) When I have a lot of experience on a subject (like HRD!), I tend to explain in too much detail and overwhelm the person I'm talking to (which can easily happen with HR jargon!).

Conclusion

When I want to implement a sustainable HRD system, whether it's in a company of 100 people or in a country of 60 million inhabitants, I keep in mind the following three factors:

1. Assessing which components of the new system to fully transfer, to modify, or to simplify
2. Finding the right counterpart
3. Supporting permanent change by using a three-phase approach (system development, training, follow up) and various methods for reducing resistance to change.

As I've mentioned previously, 15 years ago, a deputy secretary general in the Thai Ministry of Education told me, "Arnauld, in Thailand, we know *what to do* to improve. We read reports, we visit countries to learn about what others do, we have been trained by international experts; that is not the problem. Our problem is *how to implement* these new systems to be sure that they can be adapted to our Thai context."

"*How* to do is more important than *what* to do" has been my company's motto ever since.

9. FUTURE-PROOF PRODUCTION OPERATORS AND WORKERS

In 2021, I was having lunch in Bangkok with a long-term customer, who also happened to be the director of a prominent international company in the construction industry. We were discussing my LinkedIn articles, so I asked him which topic he'd like me to cover. He immediately answered, "Workers."

I wasn't surprised. He had once told me how his CEO came from France and visited one of their flagship high-rise buildings. Those constructions in Bangkok sell at the price of $7,000/m2. The CEO was impressed.

"The work quality here is better than in France!" the CEO said.

The director smiled and replied, "Could you have guessed that these buildings have been built by people who used to be farmers in the north east of Thailand, who arrived on the site without any construction knowledge?"

That is a common occurrence in Thailand.

Thai economic growth is based on millions of people who often left school at 15 years old. They are the ones who lay bricks, assemble electrical components, push the buttons of the stamping machines, and serve tourists from all over the world. These workers require basic skills training for the work to be completed successfully.

I enjoy training and developing the skills of managers, teachers, and trainers from companies, governments, and other organizations. But I am always particularly motivated by projects involving the development of workers and operators on factory machines.

In Thailand, we often see signs in front of construction sites and factories saying something like "30 workers needed." After being hired, these people are trained over one week on one task or one specific job. They might end up using the same machine or doing the same task for the next 10 years.

I have implemented three kinds of projects with great managers who were determined to develop their workers and support their career path, thinking of the process as a win-win situation. And they are right to do so: The development of workers is good for the company as well as for workers.

The first kind of project, very common in companies, is **classifying the skills of workers**.

In a construction company, we set up a system with five levels:

Level	Position	Responsibility
5	Specialist	repair defects, conduct finishing work
4	Skilled	carry out several skills and highly productive in one skill
3	Semi-skilled	carry out a skill productively (e.g., paint a certain area of wall per day)
2	Worker	carry out one skill (e.g., bricklaying or painting) following quality criteria
1	Laborer	carry loads and clean

Figure 9.1: Example 1 of classification of workers

An assessment and certification system was designed and implemented by teams of HR and production supervisors.

Workers moving up from one level to another were provided with a salary increase or skills allowance, depending on the level.

The company must systematically monitor and adjust the levels to ensure this system is sustainable because in the construction sector, the site, teams, the kind of work, and the environment change all the time.

It is easier in factories because people stay at the same site. Jobs and environments don't change all the time. So, the skills classification can be, for example:

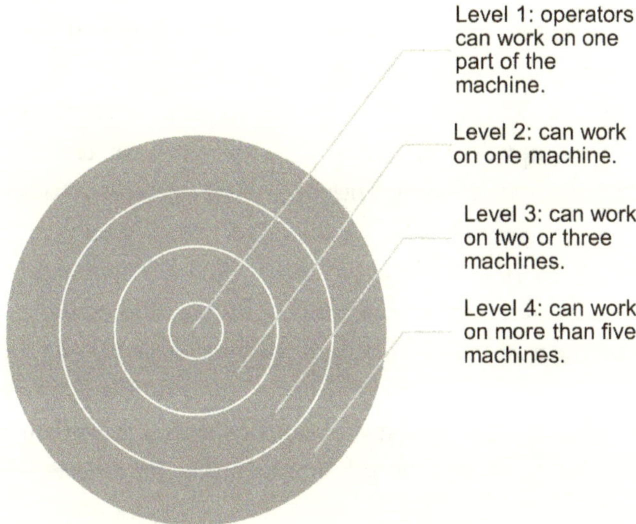

Figure 9.2: Example 2 of classification of workers

Other criteria can be used to define the levels, such as quality control, safety, or reporting.

This approach of gradual progression is valuable and necessary.

I ran one project for an international company which had a high turnover of newly-recruited production operators, despite the fact that the salary was good and the working conditions were better than in many companies (air conditioning, no noise, etc.). They wanted to understand why so many people left and how to address it. I reviewed the small tasks that they had to learn in their first week: There were more than 100! They were overwhelmed by how much they had to learn. Therefore, we adjusted the induction program and slowly introduced new skills and competencies for newcomers over the course of several months rather than all at once in the beginning.

One challenge that companies sometimes face is that many production operators, it can be up to half the workshop, don't want to leave their comfort zone, do complicated work, or have more responsibilities, despite the fact that it would enable them to become what we call "multi-skilled" and earn more money. Thus, it is essential to remind them regularly what benefits they will get.

The most complete system that I have helped to strengthen was in a factory producing ophthalmic lenses. We built a real career path for line leaders managing teams of sometimes up to 100 operators. Today, in this factory, production operators have a career path with several levels. They can grow and develop to the level of trainer, then a trainer can become a production leader of a team of operators. This position of leader has five levels based on the number of workshops they can supervise, and the most successful leaders can become supervisors. Thanks to this project, leaders understand that they can grow in the company if they leave their comfort zone and manage teams in a workshop where they have never worked as operators.

The second kind of project that I have implemented involves **the upskilling of production operators** to adapt to automation and digital technologies.

I once worked for a Thai electronics company with thousands of production operators, mainly women. Their HR manager told me, "Our operators collect information from machines. In 10 years, automation systems will do this task and all these female operators might lose their jobs."

With the support of an international organization, we built a program to train these production operators so that they could provide analysis of data collected from machines to their supervisors. The program included training on how to use Excel and PowerPoint, as well as teamwork and communication skills. It was led by teachers from the training institutes and universities, as well as a pool of supervisors who learnt how to be trainers. In the first factory, more than 1,000 operators were trained, then this project was disseminated to other Thai factories and other companies in the Association of South East Asian

Nations (ASEAN) region. These new responsibilities for the operators also had an impact on the role of their supervisors, who no longer needed to analyze data themselves. Thanks to this project, they could spend their newly-available time on more advanced tasks, supporting their manager.

These upskilling programs for operators are now developing in several countries.

The terms "upskilling" and "reskilling" are more and more used instead of the term "training."

In 2021-2022, I led a study on upskilling/reskilling in the ASEAN region by reviewing extensive international literature and presenting 10 case studies.[20] As there is no internationally-recognized definition of these two terms, we identified some characteristics that should be applied to a so-called "upskilling" or "reskilling" program.

Example of criteria for upskilling/ reskilling programs	
	1. Upskilling/reskilling to address socio-economic disruptions
	2. Integrating in technical and vocational education and training (TVET) or specific policy
	3. Using modern skills anticipation methods (forecast, foresight, big data)
	4. Defining the target group (e.g., mainly female workers, with education not higher than technician level)
	5. Integrating a set of skills (core, functional, cognitive) to get significant job change
	6. Modalities of implementation in three phases: 1) preparation; 2) monitoring; 3) support, including financial if self-employed
	7. Learning process with various modalities: group training, internet-based, work-based, individual coaching
	8. Recognizing skills with a modular approach (credits, unit of competency, micro-credentials, new level of classification)
	9. Monitoring and evaluation of the program at different levels (satisfaction, learning, behavior, impact)
	10. Financing using various means and partnerships

Figure 9.3: List of criteria for upskilling or reskilling

The third kind of project to enhance the prospects of workers or production operators is preparing them for future jobs through **apprenticeships.**

---

20 GIZ. (2023). *Reskilling and Upskilling in ASEAN Through a Gender Lens.* Recotvet,

In Thailand, it's called "dual vocational training." Around 20% of vocational education students learn with this approach. I have helped a jewelry company recruit 20 students aged 15 to 20 each year as apprentices. Over the course of three years, they spend one day per week in a vocational education school to get a vocational certificate degree. During this period, students receive an allowance and get free accommodation. They later can be recruited, or not, as technicians. In theory, everybody wins.

The process is as below.

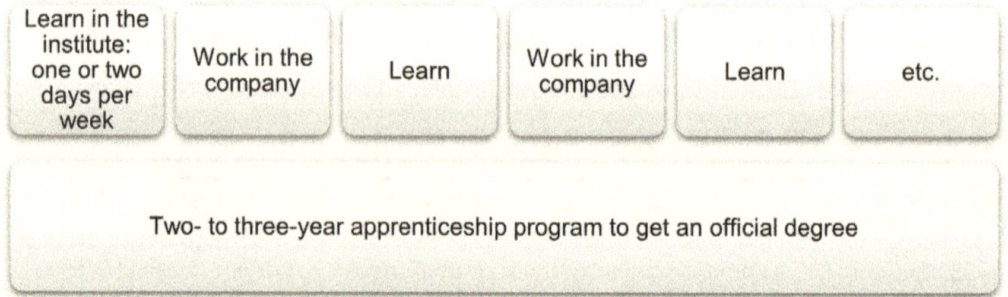

Figure 9.4: Synthesis of the apprenticeship model

But, this project is not as easy to implement as it seems. There are several issues:

- The company must develop students' skills and not limit them to basic jobs like cleaning tools for three years.
- The teacher must follow up on students' work to ensure that what they learn corresponds to the curriculum that they follow in the institute.
- Students must be mature enough to adapt to the culture shock of going from living with grandparents in small provincial cities to a dormitory in Bangkok's suburbs.

Conclusion

Ultimately, having skilled labor to support investment and economic development plans is a pressing issue in Thailand and many other countries for three main reasons:

1. Young people are increasingly rejecting industrial jobs where they have to work under pressure from the boss (fixed working time, performance to deliver) and in working conditions that can be difficult (heat, noise, dirtiness). This became more acute during and after the COVID-19 pandemic.

2. Thailand is among several countries, especially in Asia, with a rapidly ageing population. In 2050, there will be 1.7 productive people upon whom one older person can depend. That number was seven in 2000.

3. At the same time, jobs are changing as technology advances. An article by The Asia Foundation mentions that, "More than 50 percent of work activities in Malaysia, Indonesia, India, and Thailand have the potential for automation."[21]

Governments are trying to address this issue of a dwindling workforce. Under an agreement (Memorandum of Understanding) with Myanmar, Lao PDR, and Cambodia, Thailand receives more than three million migrants. It is a valuable boost to the unskilled workforce, but not enough to provide the qualified workers needed.

Thus, in the end, it is up to companies to implement development programs such as apprenticeships, classification, and upskilling that will enable their staff to carry out the jobs of today and tomorrow. And if these students and adult workers accept the constraints of industrial jobs and are willing to go out of their comfort zone, they will have opportunities to grow and develop, with more responsibilities and income.

---

21 The Asia Foundation (2020). *The Fourth Industrial Revolution and the Future of Work*. p.23 https://asiafoundation.org/publication/ the-fourth-industrial-revolution-and-the-future-of-work-implications-for-asian-development-cooperation/

10. SO MANY KINDS OF CUSTOMERS OR POTENTIAL ONES

I'm not a salesperson. When HR companies ask me to promote and sell their product and service, I always decline.

But I still need to sell myself and my services to potential customers. Thus, in this chapter, I want to shine a light on the situations I face.

I have two main types of customer:

- International organizations, education companies, and governments for projects outside Thailand
- Companies

I will focus this chapter on the second category, although there are parallels with the first.

Since 2005, I have implemented more than 100 HRD projects, both training and consulting, bringing value (I hope) to more than 50 companies or factories in Thailand.

During all these years, I have come across four different kinds of customer:

1. Long-term customers who hire for a "full scope of expertise"

There are around 10 companies with which I have run HRD projects over the course of several years. These customers regularly ask me to improve various parts of their HRD systems using my expertise (performance, competency, training, etc.). They trust that I will provide the best service as I know their needs, context, and teams. As we have built a relationship over the years, I often give more than they expect, and I might even reduce my costs if the work has been implemented quicker than planned.

2. Long-term customers who hire for one expertise

This type of customer needs one specific expertise once a year, which is always the same. For example, measuring the return on investment of training. They trust that I will provide the best service. Again, I know their needs, context, and teams, and I often give more than they expect. As they have a specific vision of what I can bring, it is sometimes difficult to offer them the full scope of my expertise. If I did, they would fall into the above category.

3. Potential long-term customers after one project

In this case, the customer and I successfully implement a first project together. Trust is built. We keep in touch, and we hope, especially me, to collaborate in the future, which sometimes happens. Once, I did a six-month training project for a construction company working in partnership with an HR supervisor. After the project ended, I contacted his manager, but nothing happened. Then, three years later, while I was driving one Saturday afternoon, I received a call from this supervisor who had become a manager in another company. He asked me if I was still doing training projects because he needed my support. I was very surprised, but it was the beginning of a long-term cooperation (he now falls into the first category).

4. One-shot customers

They hire me for one specific expertise. Then they ask for more: "Can you also do this? Can you reduce the price? There will be other projects in the future!" I'm sure you have encountered this in your own line of work. I end up giving more than what was planned in the hope that there will be other projects. But, more often than not, after the contract ends, there is no more contact, even if the customer seemed satisfied. They got what they wanted.

And then there are the potential ones, those who got away, and don't hire me for various reasons.

The ones who are always asking me to add more and more information to my proposal (templates, free sessions, examples), but it ends with "we will contact you." They think they can do everything by themselves now that they have all the information that I provided, free of charge, of course.

The ones for whom I started to work without having a contract signed, thinking that trust had been built (the Asian way). But then, they end up telling me that there isn't enough budget to pay me. Luckily, this scenario is rare.

The ones who don't hire me because I don't offer a fancy, attractive "one size fits all" solution (a ready-to-use training package, the perfect list of competencies, etc.) to their complex problems. Many HR partners expect that providers, especially foreign ones, have a perfect, off-the-shelf package ready to go. I remember one instance when I started as a consultant in Thailand and I got a meeting with the HR director of a large conglomerate. She asked me, "What do you propose?" Proudly, I gave a customer-focused answer, "I don't propose anything, but I'm here to listen to your needs." After a long discussion, she finally expressed a vague need to develop her internal trainers, but it wasn't enough for a project. This helped me later understand what it means when people say, "They don't know what they don't know."

The ones to whom I failed to show the value of my proposal, or they couldn't see how I would add value to their existing system. That's fair enough.

The ones who have their own network of consultants. I was once introduced to a company which wanted to define a competency system but was not sure whether to use a consultant or do it internally. Based on several discussions, I prepared a detailed proposal with several options. They concluded by telling me that they will do the work by themselves (I assumed probably using some of the methods I proposed). I contacted them three months later. The HR representative told me that, instead of defining the competency system by themselves or asking me to support them, they finally hired an expensive consultant who knew one of the company executives. As you might imagine, I felt downhearted.

The ones who don't hire me because the name of my company is not as well-known as others, such as EY or Deloitte. This reason was once given by the HR vice president of a large Thai industrial group with whom I had already collaborated on eight projects. When we stopped working together, he explained to me that the group policy was now to select only well-known consulting firms because then, in case of failure, management could argue it wasn't their fault as they had selected one of the best in the world.

The ones that I call "my competitors." These are HR managers who are not so interested in seeking support from consultants because they don't want to ask their CEO for a budget and risk getting the answer, "Why do you need an external consultant to improve our HRD system? That's your job." I remember I had this situation with a company where I met the CEO and HR director who were interested in my support, but I made the mistake of not involving the training manager who did not see the need and had more power than I thought. Then, I did not implement any project.

The ones that I call the "ghost customers." I meet them at a social event, we have a great discussion, they seem very interested and say, "Please recontact me next month." But when I contact them, they don't answer;

they just disappear. When this happens, I can't help but wonder if our discussion was a dream. Having lived nearly 30 years in Thailand, I know that many Thai people don't like to say no, but I remain very frustrated when I do not know if my emails or messages are in their spam box or they are just not interested and do not want to tell me the reasons.

And lastly, we have the ones that I don't want to work for, for ethical reasons. I was once contacted via email by the HR manager of a very large Burmese company. They asked if we could meet online to discuss their HRD needs. I was excited; it seemed exactly within my scope of expertise, until I had a talk with my Burmese housemaid. She told me that this company was supported by the current military dictatorship. Taken aback, I looked for more information on the matter; it was true. I replied to the HR manager that I wouldn't have time to work with them.

In order to turn potential customers into real ones, I identify several components that I try to integrate (although not always successfully).

Figure 10.1: Components needed to transform prospects to customers

The "selling process" has to take into account all the other parameters.

I remember discovering a powerful selling process when I facilitated some training in Thailand implemented by an American organization. Their sales approach was based on:

- A deep analysis of the customer context (profile, objectives, issues, strategies to address issues)
- Identification of people who might support or gatekeepers who might resist our proposal
- Communication to decision-makers based on their business needs

It was a powerful model, although not always easy to implement.

Conclusion

So, as you can see, there are a myriad of potential customers for a consultant. I won't get bored, that's for sure. And often, I don't always know which kind of customer they are until I am dealing with them. Sometimes, I think they are lost and suddenly they appear again; other times, I think that we are at the beginning of a long-term cooperation, but nothing happens, or they disappear.

If I want to transfer a prospect to customer, then, just like cooking a meal, I need to find the right mix of ingredients from their business needs, their demand, my capacity to answer, their own challenges, and the image that they have of what I can bring. The selling process will have to integrate all these components to create the ideal recipe. I have friends who are sales experts and can find the right mix immediately. For me, it's a constant learning curve; but practice makes perfect, and eventually I will improve and make those that got away part of my loyal customer base.

11. MATCHING TRAINING DEMANDS AND NEEDS

In 1995, when I was a young trainer in France, I organized a successful training program for a sales team in a company that produced furniture. The HR manager of another company belonging to the same industrial group asked me, "Arnauld, I heard that your training in our affiliate company was successful; can you do the same for our sales team?"

I launched the program in his company right away. After the first session, his sales team told me, "It's a nice training session, but it's not exactly what we want."

In my past 35 years as a consultant, manager, or team leader implementing HRD projects, I have often faced situations where the *demand* from the client doesn't correspond to their real *need*.

My understanding of the initial demand may not match the real needs of the company and its staff (e.g., the sales team in the case mentioned above), which are often more complex.

The demand is often expressed in a simple way, but the real needs happen to be much more complex.

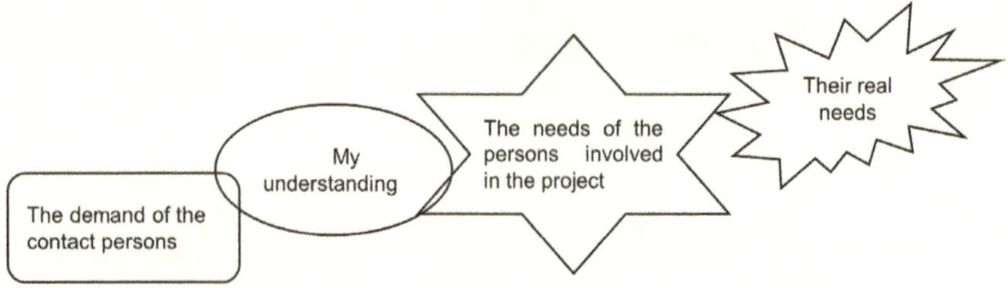

Figure 11.1: From simple demand to complex needs

Below are some examples of when I might face such a situation:

Case 1: Mismatch of intervention concept

In this scenario, for example, I receive training requests from HR managers who want their managers "to be better leaders" when, in fact, the real need is more specific, such as better organization or better communication. To avoid this issue, whenever there is a training request, my main question is, "What business impact do you expect from this training?" Their answer helps me clarify their real needs so I can propose a different method to solve the problem if needs be.

I remember using this approach for a management training project. The initial request was for a day or two of training on "performance management." The project became "supporting and coaching managers on how to implement a performance management system with regular one-to-one meetings." It was successful and the client was satisfied.

Case 2: Mismatch of topic

In this case, I might have a CEO with a clear idea of what training content they want, whereas the trainees are expecting something different. In this kind of situation, I have to juggle these two needs: delivering the CEO's message while adjusting the content of the training to also take into account the participants' needs.

Case 3: No need

Here, the manager is paying for people to be trained on something they don't feel they need. The HR manager of a Thai bank once asked me to measure the efficiency and impact of their English language training employees working in branches where there were hardly any foreign customers. You can imagine that the return on investment was very low as, without foreigners to interact with, they had no opportunity to practice their new skills. But, in this case, the training was not completely useless. I told my customer that a financial return on investment is not everything. Some training is about developing employees' understanding of new concepts and visions. In this case, this English language training helped the bank create an international culture.

Case 4: The hidden need

A few years ago, a friend of mine was sent by his company, a large Thai group, to Harvard University in the US for a one-month training program. After he came back, I asked him, "What elements of your training program do you think you will apply at work?" He couldn't really answer but, instead, he replied, "You know, the situation in Thailand is different, but it was a great session and I really enjoyed it." Officially, his company sent him because they needed him to develop leadership skills to apply at work, but the hidden goal was to reward him. I found that this approach is often used by companies willing to keep their top talents.

Case 5: Unrealistic demands

Sometimes, I have to try and meet unrealistic demands. I remember an instance when I was assigned to plan a teacher-training development program for an international organization which provided a large loan to an Asian country. The government of this country had planned to spend many millions of US dollars to buy new equipment for teacher-training institutes and to train thousands of teachers using it. I explained to them that there was a risk that these teachers would not apply the knowledge gained in their school after training because this new equipment was not installed. The government seemed to have missed the concept of "start with the end in mind." Indeed, the plan should have been to improve the programs and equipment used by the students, and only afterwards develop the skills of teachers with the same equipment.

For me, this was an example of when the demand of the government doesn't match the real needs of the people concerned. When this situation arises, I try to negotiate with my counterpart in order to avoid the failure of a project for which I might later be partly responsible. With this project, I did so by supporting the quick training of teachers on the existing equipment and adding installation of new equipment in the schools.

Case 6: Changing needs

Sometimes, the people who make the request simply ... change their minds. I once did a six-month project preparing a vocational training strategy for the Ministry of Education of an Asian country. The result is normally a 30- to 40-page document. I did what I usually do, which is to try and validate the table of contents with the client as early as possible to ensure common understanding of the structure of the document before writing out the details. After his validation, I travelled every month to that country and spent time reviewing the structure of the document with the representative of the organization funding this assignment. Over the course of regular meetings, we made some adjustments to the document. My partner seemed satisfied. He used to tell me, "If the ministry is happy, then I'm happy." Nevertheless, when I submitted the 40-page draft report at the end, I was surprised to hear him say, "I'm sorry, but this isn't what I want." I was downcast and ended up having to change nearly a third of the document. I wondered what I could have done differently to be aware of his change of vision.

Case 7: Demands follow budget

In multi-million-dollar projects supported by international organizations or European governments, we must be very careful about what the real need is. A lot of money is at stake. If I were to simply ask local partners, "Do you need to change the equipment in your training centers?" most of the time they will reply yes, even if it might not be the priority. Developing countries tend to accept what donors offer even if it isn't their real need, a priority, or even included in their overall strategy or development plan.

As demonstrated, there are many situations where demands can be disconnected from the actual needs. It is strange that, when I Googled "methods to align demand and need," I couldn't find any relevant result, except my own article on LinkedIn. Everything else focused on matching demand and supply.

When I face these various situations, I try to use five methods to align demands and needs.

Method 1: Negotiate

Sometimes, local counterparts do express their needs. Let me use an example. In Vietnam, I was once team leader of a large project where I had a monthly project management meeting with the representatives of the Ministry of Labor. We had very lengthy discussions about the way to implement the project and agreeing my usual 40-slide PowerPoint review presentation – 30 hours over the course of five days was the longest time we spent. I remember finishing the week exhausted. But I got to really understand their real needs.

Method 2: Ask open questions

When I work in foreign countries like Bangladesh or Uzbekistan, we all are non-native English speakers. I'm often not sure what they understand or don't understand from my "Frenglish." Asking open questions is a good way to know what they really know. I try to avoid questions such as, "Do you understand?" or, "Is it clear?" as in some countries people might say yes just to make you happy. Indeed, I once sat next to a consultant who was explaining to the Vietnamese director of a vocational college the benefits of organizing training for companies. He spoke nearly non-stop for an hour. I really wondered what the director understood and agreed with. Therefore, I try to ask questions such as, "What are the kinds of priorities that you have for the next three years?" and, "How are you going to address them?"

Working in Thailand, either in English or Thai, people often don't speak up during my training session when I asked participants if they understood the assignment. But when I split them into smaller groups, I discover that some of the participants do not understand either the theory that had been taught or the assignment, despite me asking. It's one of the many culture shocks I have been subjected to working in Asia. I found this to be quite common in Thailand. Trainees don't say that they don't know for three reasons: 1) They do not lose face by asking questions in front of their colleagues; 2) Trainers are happy because they think everybody understood; and 3) Trainees avoid the risk of making the trainers lose face if they cannot answer the questions.

Method 3: Double check answers

I often ask the same questions to several people to get confirmation. This works particularly well when I implement projects such as customer need analysis, project review, or evaluation. For example, I would ask the director of a vocational school, "How are you involved in the development of the curriculum?" and, the day after, I would ask the representative of the ministry, "How do you involve directors of schools in the creation of a new curriculum?"

Method 4: Use data

When I did my certification program on how to measure the return on investment of HRD programs, my trainer would always say "show me the data." When I review, evaluate, or analyze a situation, need, or program, I'm dealing with people who have a lot of ideas and opinions. It's important to corroborate these opinions with data from relevant literature and the report review.

Method 5: Meet people individually

I tend to spend a lot of time producing nice documents which I'm proud to send to my partners, only to be disappointed when I realize that they didn't read them or I discover, sometimes too late, that they don't agree with some parts of it. Even though it's their fault as they should have read my reports, I'm still responsible. In a previous chapter, I mentioned that one way to make people accept a change (e.g., new methodology or system) or the results of an evaluation or study is to explain it bit by bit over the course of the project and not wait until the end to suddenly present the complete document. Therefore, meeting people individually to explain what I do or what changes might happen will give them a better understanding of the real needs and how I propose to meet them.

I sum up below these five methods that will help match demand and needs.

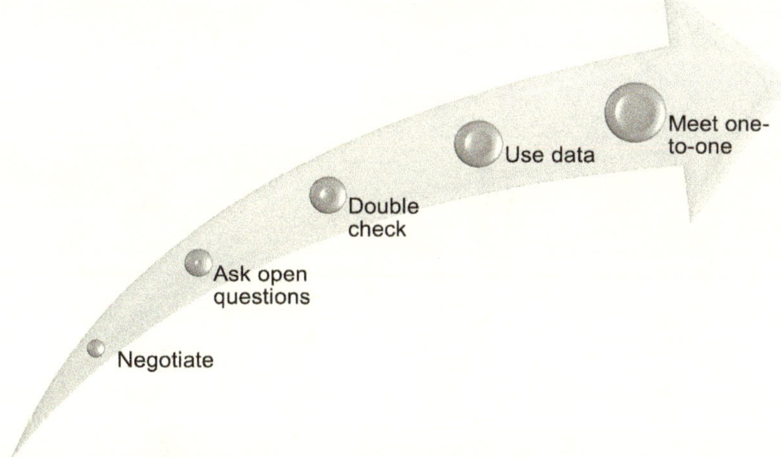

Figure 11.2: Five methods to go from a simple demand to real needs

Conclusion

Despite having these five methods at my disposal to unearth any hidden objectives, it remains a challenge to mitigate the risk of failing to meet a client's needs.

When I published a LinkedIn article on this topic of demands and needs, a friend commented that systematic approaches are used these days, such as the "design thinking" method. This is a non-linear, iterative process that teams use to understand customers, challenge assumptions, redefine problems, and create innovative solutions to then prototype and test. It involves five phases – empathize, define, ideate, prototype, and test. It seems an innovative approach, although I think I sometimes use this process (or parts of it) without giving it this name. But I feel that it can work if the partner/customer is willing to participate and isn't just waiting for *the* solution to be brought by the consultants, especially if they are foreigners.

12. GETTING BUSINESS AND EDUCATION TO SPEAK A COMMON LANGUAGE

In 2021, as a member of a foreign chamber of commerce in Thailand, I was at a meeting of its HRD committee. The participants were complaining about the difficulty of adapting the skills of the Thai workforce to the so-called "Industry 4.0" (Fourth Industrial Revolution).

It was a brainstorming session: Should we have some training programs? But for which target group? The youth? The unemployed? Workers? How can we do that? Which skills do we want to develop? Do we need to cooperate with the Ministry of Education? Or should we set up our own training center or a direct partnership with a selected institute?

These questions revealed the company representatives' frustration about the capacity of training and education institutions to provide a workforce with suitable knowledge and skills.

The importance of partnerships between companies and education institutes is well known. One traditional example is when a company provides education scholarships to selected talents or people with potential. But there are many other ways to cooperate.

Based on my experience of working with both companies and governments, I proposed some questions to answer to try and find a better balance of demand and supply of workers.

If companies want to cooperate with education institutes (initial vocational education colleges or continuing skills development centers), they must address these questions:

1. What *socio-economic issues or disruptions* are we facing? That can include new technology, the evolution of the labor market, change of products, evolution of customer needs, new environmental constraints, restructuring of the organization, etc.

2. *What is the target group?* I've found that companies usually have two kinds of issues:
    ♦   The company can't find and recruit qualified workers; or, when they do, they don't have the fundamental knowledge (numeracy, literacy), core skills (teamwork, problem solving, digital skills, etc.), or functional skills (painting, sewing, mechanics, etc.) needed.
    ♦   The company has a workforce that lacks this fundamental knowledge and core or functional skills: they don't speak English, they don't know how to use the machines, how to repair an electrical motor, how to work in teams, how to solve problems, etc.

3. After we select the target groups to focus on, we can decide: Do we want to develop or recruit specific occupations, such as maintenance technician or skilled construction worker, or do we want to provide core or fundamental knowledge and skills to be used in any kind of occupation? After making this choice, we can define more precisely the *three types of skills and knowledge:*
    ♦   Cognitive: literacy, numeracy, foreign languages, digital literacy
    ♦   Core: communication, time management, problem solving, etc.
    ♦   Functional: specific to each occupation, like repairing electrical motors or accounting.

4. Then, we need to address the important issue of recognition. How do we recognize the achievement at the end of the program? This can be:

    ◆ An official certification recognized by a public authority: For instance, in Thailand, that would be a certification from the Ministry of Education (vocational certificate, higher technician), Ministry of Labor (skills standards), or Thai Professional Qualification Institute (professional qualification).

    ◆ A training institute certificate that might not be officially recognized nor connected to the national qualification framework.

5. When we are clear on the target, we review the *education and training supply:* which institute delivers what and for whom? Is it enough? Does it meet our needs?

6. Finally, we *decide what we do*: Do we create a new institute? That can be in the form of a training center, private vocational education college, or university. Or just cooperate with existing ones?

After going through this process, we then need to determine what kind of partnership we want.

If companies, federations, and training or education institutes want to cooperate, how could they do so? I have implemented and participated in **nine kinds of partnerships** to support the development of the workforce.

The company can:

1. *Use trainers and institute facilities for short training programs:* I once organized a program on maintenance over several weeks with a university, with the purpose of strengthening the theoretical knowledge of the company technicians. It worked because the teachers were able to understand the company's needs and context. But, in another country, I organized the same kind of partnership

with the most well-known technical college in the country. Unfortunately, the project failed because the teachers didn't set a good example: they came late, provided unclear and poorly prepared documents, their lectures overran and weren't relatable to the experience of the workers. I might have been too naïve in the selection of the partner.

2. *Use trainers and institute facilities for training on site:* Many years ago, I helped to organize 10-day courses on brick-laying, tiling, and plastering for construction workers. The course was followed by a three-hour assessment. This project succeeded because the HR manager and I reviewed very precisely the method and content of the course delivered by the training institute. Moreover, the training took place within a building that was being constructed.

3. *Provide scholarships for education degrees:* Large companies often offer scholarships to selected people with potential, in the hope that the person will stay after their studies. Even though that's not always the case, this shows the dedication of the company to education. I especially like it when companies support low-skilled workers. I remember working with a Japanese company which was funding the cost of a vocational education degree for 20 workers, which took place every weekend for three years. I was impressed by the support of the company and the workers' motivation.

4. *Hire students for internships or apprenticeships:* Many companies are willing to receive a couple of students over the course of several months. But to make this process work, firstly, a good follow-up from teachers is essential to ensure the students learn, practice, and don't end up making photocopies or serving the coffee. Secondly,

success depends on students' level of autonomy. For example, I remember talking with a friend of mine, the CEO of a small company which had three French interns. "How different are they from Thai students?" I asked. He replied, "It's a whole different world; they're very good in terms of technique, but I especially appreciate that they challenge me, propose new ideas, and don't hesitate to share their concerns about our work and project."

5. *Conduct research projects in collaboration with the institute:* They can be implemented by a variety of students. Even with vocational education, it is possible to make a valuable contribution to the company. I remember visiting a Thai company with a French vocational education college teacher. He showed me several small mechanisms and automated installations and told me, "These kinds of systems can be done by students in their final project assignment."

6. *Send engineers and managers from the company to give short training sessions for students in the education institute:* This approach is interesting as it forces company staff to build a pedagogical package and to learn how to teach. Then they can apply these skills to their own work.

7. *Adjust the existing curriculum of a vocational education college or university to the needs of the company:* Depending on the country, national higher or vocational education curricula has some flexibility to be adjusted to the needs of companies (usually in their elective subjects), around 5%-20% of the full program. I have had the opportunity to coordinate this kind of work where teachers and engineers sit together and identify the competencies needed, review the curriculum, and decide on new content. This can work if the company is large enough to receive a certain number of students (e.g., 15) or if a

cluster of companies working in the same field is set up.

8. *Provide equipment to the education institute:* The most common situation is when the company gives away its old equipment to an institute because new technology is needed for their production process. But the company might also provide hi-tech machines or systems if the institute is willing to promote its equipment. One key condition of success is to ensure that the equipment provided is suitable for the curriculum, i.e., it is the right technology and there is enough for all students. For five years, I was the deputy director of a center promoting French technology in a Thai university. Some equipment donated did not meet these criteria, so it was never used and just gathered dust.

9. *Create its own training/education facilities with the cooperation of public or private institute teachers:* This can be small scale, e.g., setting up a few rooms in the existing institute and dedicating them to training on the company technology or process. Companies can also go bigger with a new multi-million-dollar dedicated training center, including all the relevant equipment, trainers, administrative staff, management, etc., supported by the education institute or the ministry in charge. The partnership must be well defined and agreed upon. I once did a feasibility study to create a national training center in the clothing industry. After several years of fruitless discussions between the industry association and the Ministry of Labor about how it would work, the former finally decided to build and manage this center on their own.

As we see, the process is straightforward.

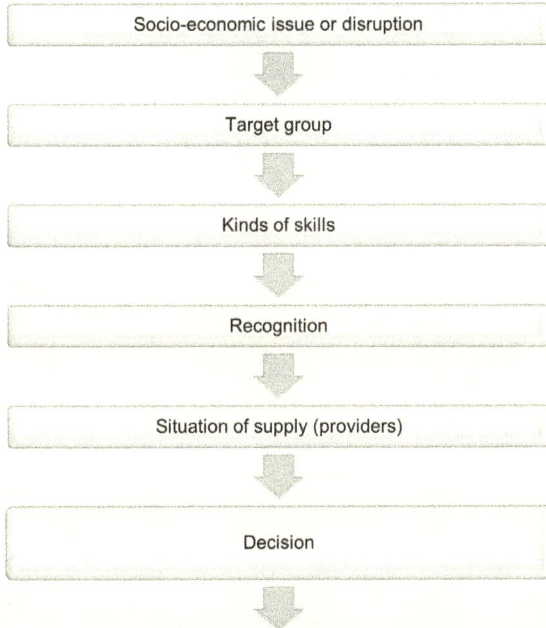

Figure 12.1: Seven steps to build long term partnerships between education and business

But in practice, it is not always easy to make company staff or managers work with teachers and directors of vocational schools or universities. They have different needs, challenges, issues, and constraints. A formal agreement and related action plans must be written to define expected outcomes, their corresponding activities, resources needed, roles and responsibilities, and an evaluation system.

Conclusion

To guarantee having a workforce with suitable skills, companies must precisely define the scope of their needs from the top. Then, if a partnership with an institute is the solution, both organizations can sit together to establish what they want to do to ensure a long-term, win-win cooperation, using some of the nine possible approaches listed above that will help develop workers with the skills needed for the industry of the present and the future.

13. VOCATIONAL EDUCATION SYSTEMS: HOW TO SUCCEED WITH IMPROVEMENT

I've talked about how companies and educational institutes can cooperate to support the development of the workforce. Now I want to share the conditions needed for these vocational education and training projects to be successful, both now and for years to come.

I have had the chance to implement more than 30 government projects to support the improvement of vocational education and training systems in 11 Asian countries. They were financially supported by an international organization (e.g., Asian Development Bank, UNESCO, International Labour Organization) or a specific country (e.g. Germany, France, Switzerland).

However, when I reflect on my past assignments, I find myself thinking, *How is the Cambodian institute that I helped to create doing? Was my Thai-French competency-based project really successful? What remains from that $30 million project in Lao PDR? What about all these French training programs transferred to Vietnam? Did the Marshall Islands government implement the HRD plan that we prepared together?*

Below, I have categorized my interventions using four levels, with their specific conditions to succeed.

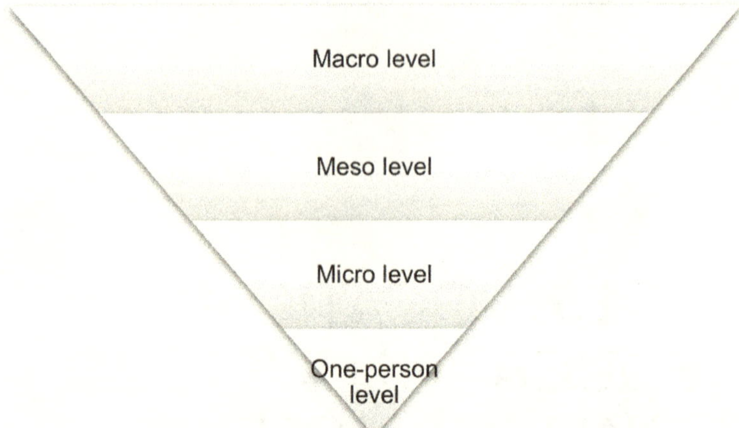

Figure 13.1: Four kinds of interventions to improve vocational education

Macro-level intervention

This is the implementation of a large, national project that impacts many aspects of an institute (e.g., program change, policy review, purchasing new equipment, construction of building, etc.).

In this situation, the development partner gives a loan or a grant of tens of millions of dollars, and there could be a large number of institutes involved. Most of the time, the project includes improving the training system in specific sectors, such as clothing or construction, and providing new buildings, equipment, or teacher training. They might also provide scholarships or dormitories for trainees. A team from the ministry leads the project. It's an effective way to get quick results thanks to the input of teams of consultants and the support of the ministry concerned. However, they do not always fully attain the expected results.

At first, I believe four conditions need to be met in order to succeed.:

♦ The planning and implementation phases should be clearly split. I remember a project where we had to rush to prepare the list of equipment before the programs were even selected. There should be three main phases: opportunity study, feasibility study or planning, and implementation.

- ◊ The opportunity study defines business needs, supply and demand of skills, governmental priorities, expected recognition linked to programs, etc.
- ◊ The feasibility study details the planning, the definition of methodologies to review or to create programs, the budget, the terms of reference to recruit an implementation agency, the equipment needed, etc.
- ◊ The implementation phase includes the transfer or adjustment of all programs, the training of teachers and managers, the installation of equipment, coaching, and mentoring to support implementation, and all other activities as defined in the feasibility study.

♦ The training programs being strengthened should consider socio-economic needs as well as students' motivation. Let me illustrate. I once worked on a project aimed at improving the training programs in the construction sector. However, the number of new vocational education students in the whole country, annually, was less than 200 (yes, you read that right). There was a clear mismatch between the motivation of the youth and economic needs. To attract more students, a more popular program on business and marketing was added. Budgets for scholarships and promotion campaigns were also included.

♦ The institute partners should be carefully selected based on: 1) the readiness and motivation of managers and teachers to change; and 2) their financial and time constraints. I once led a team of consultants which implemented a project including the provision of new equipment and improvement of training programs. We discovered during the project that the school was very interested in the former but not the latter.

♦ Change must be progressive. The existing methods, habits,

and knowledge of managers and teachers must be considered when implementing any new systems, programs, or teaching methods. We can't change 20 years of habits in a five-day training session. I think that the development partner often acts as a link between the ministry motivated by innovative, modern approaches and what is really feasible at the institute level. I remember one project I worked for, implemented in a country ranked lower than 130th in terms of development which wanted new programs on cybersecurity and mechatronics akin to those in Singapore. Closing the gap seemed unrealistic to me.

Meso-level intervention

This is a small-scale project with local institutes or a ministry. Teams of international experts and local teachers work together to create and/or implement new systems, curricula, and training methods.

This approach often works as it's feasible and relatively easy to set up teams and budgets. This is how many non-governmental organizations work.

In this kind of project, matching limited financial resources to the needs and context of the organization is essential. I remember one project where the initial plan of the development partner was to organize a series of seminars on what a good vocational training system should be. During the feasibility study, I met the various stakeholders and was able to identify a more urgent need: creating a quality system for TVET institutes. I suggested to the development partner that we could make better use of the budget by supporting this project rather than paying for seminars, which we did. The quality system was created, and I felt that our help had been valuable because it was impacting institutes across the whole country.

One challenge for small-scale projects is to ensure dissemination and sustainability.

To address this problem, the ministry or organization concerned must, of course, be regularly involved and the mechanism for future replication and sustainability should be prepared. For this, using the framework of an existing quality system can help.

In 2020, I worked on a project that created guidelines to check the gender sensitivity and inclusiveness of training courses. I wasn't sure they would really be used at the end of my assignment. However, at the final meeting, the director of the relevant department declared that these guidelines would be forwarded to the quality system division. I was suddenly much more hopeful about the sustainability of this project. Transferring systems, methods, and guidelines into procedures and internal quality systems is a good way to support long-term results.

Micro-level intervention

This could be the creation of a new institute (or complete restructuring of an existing one).

In this situation, the development partner supports the creation of a national center, institute, or academy in a specific sector with a multi-million-dollar investment. Starting from scratch might seem easier than overhauling programs, equipment, and HR in an existing institute. But there are risks to this approach, as organization constraints (especially relating to budgets), reluctance to change, and insufficient knowledge and skills of the managers and trainers could all present barriers.

For this kind of project, I must ensure the return on investment of the project: What happens when the international support ends? What will be the impact on staff salaries? How will the equipment be maintained? Will the center be able to generate enough income to be sustainable? Will there be turnover of important staff, especially when the support of development partners ends? And so on.

One way to mitigate the risks is to involve the private sector (companies, associations, federations) and set up a public private partnership

(PPP) with the ministry concerned in order to share cost and resources. In this situation, the modalities of management and operation of the institute must be precisely defined and agreed.

One-person-level intervention

This is very focused, like bringing in an international advisor to a ministry or a national organization.

In this situation, an international expert such as myself is assigned to an office in the local organization, whether that is an institute, a government department, or a professional federation. One challenge that I have seen (and lived!) is when the organization where the experts are based provides them with a nice office and a fancy title, but the local staff rarely ask them any questions or involve them in daily management and activities.

Thus, I believe several conditions need to be met to make this arrangement successful:

1. The expert must have an official counterpart in the organization and clear deliverables on an identified challenge (e.g., change of law, setting up standards, developing a methodology). The definition of the assignment shouldn't be too generalized, e.g., "Our international advisor will advise the local team on how to develop their vocational education system."
2. Speaking the local language surely helps if the international expert is going to participate in meetings and make informal connections with people.
3. The capacity to build trusting relationships with local staff is essential. For this, the expert should have good communication skills (e.g., asking questions, giving feedback) and be mindful of the local culture.

4. And some personality traits like curiosity of other cultures, patience, and humility help them to accept others and be accepted.

I sum up below these four ways to develop vocational education systems with the corresponding actions needed.

Four ways to improve vocational education systems	National reform	Adopt a three-phase approach
		Align motivation of trainees/students to socio-economic needs
		Pick the right partners
		Use existing methods
	Local intervention	Match limited financial resources to real needs
		Use quality systems (if they exist)
	Support to institute	Prepare sustainability; start small
		Involve private sector
	Advisory assignment	Define deliverables with local counterpart
		Speak the local language
		Communication skills
		Personality traits (curiosity, humility, patience)

Figure 13.2: Four ways to develop vocational education systems and conditions to succeed

Conclusion

I described above various conditions in each of my four approaches: macro level (national reform), meso level (local intervention), micro level (support to institute) and "one-person" level (advisory assignment). In fact, all these conditions can be applied to any of these four approaches. Moreover, they are not just specific to vocational education but can be applied to all kinds of projects.

Regardless of the size or nature of the intervention, whether it's a new multi-million-dollar international training center or one expert at a desk in an organization, success is dependent on some common factors. Implementing these will ensure that your project makes a difference not just at the time, but for years to come.

PART 3:

KNOWLEDGE, SKILLS, AND CAPACITIES NEEDED TO SUCCESSFULLY IMPLEMENT THESE SYSTEMS

14. SKILLS NEEDED TO KEEP MY JOB

For more than 30 years, I have enjoyed developing the skills of other people as a consultant and trainer for governments, international organizations, and companies.

It made me think about the skills that I need to have, and I found that there are six that are really important for me, either as a trainer or as consultant.

1. Asking questions

A few years ago, while I was working in Lao PDR, I met with a director of an institute in the Ministry of Education, and he told me, "Arnauld, you aren't like other consultants I worked with; you don't always tell us what we have to do."

I took it as a compliment even if, to this day, I'm still unsure if he meant it that way.

I believe that the most important skill for a consultant is to ask questions. I have had assignments in countries as diverse as the Marshall Islands and Pakistan. Different places have different histories, contexts, visions, and needs. Asking questions to understand these elements is essential before I can offer any feasible recommendations to improve their HRD system.

I'm not always good at asking questions. But I have been in meetings with some consultants who would only ask our partners two or three questions before starting to explain what to do or sharing their experience from other countries. I remember one consultant explaining in detail to representatives of a ministry in Cambodia how successful he was in Ivory Coast, in Africa. I really felt uncomfortable.

When I start a new assignment and hold my first meetings with a partner or a customer, I keep in mind the following ratio: 80%-90% asking open questions as much as possible about their purpose, objective, structure, challenges, needs, etc.; and the remaining 10%-20% sharing my experience and knowledge to demonstrate that I can bring value.

2. Public speaking

For the past 30 years, I have had to explain, train, and make speeches in front of audiences of all sizes. To be effective, I must be impactful.

I stopped counting the number of events at which there were poor public speeches. You know which ones I'm talking about; the audience are either sleeping, confused, or playing with their smartphones. We have all witnessed these behaviors, and let's admit it, we've also been guilty of them.

I remember once that a director of an international company in Thailand gave such a poor speech at the annual meeting that it probably cost him the election to the board. I'm bewildered that today, still, there are leaders and consultants who don't seem to know the basics of public speaking.

I believe that I continuously need to develop so, as I mentioned previously, for the past five years I have been a member of the public speaking association Toastmasters International.[22] We meet regularly, practice public speaking, evaluate and are evaluated based on: structuring the content using key points, engaging the audience, keeping eye contact, demonstrating positive body language, ensuring variety in tone and speed, cutting out useless words, and respecting the time allocated. I'm committed to improving, but this is a never-ending project.

22 https://www.toastmasters.org/

3. Giving feedback

As a consultant-trainer-coach, I need to give corrective feedback to trainees, partners, and customers either by speaking or writing. It can be difficult.

I use three main methods:

- Direct feedback (either positive or corrective) based on precise facts and behaviors followed by the impact. For example, "I was confused due to the lack of structure in your report. I do not see clearly what you delivered at the end of the project. How could you make it more precise?" Or, for the positive feedback, "Your questions were very precise, which enabled us to write all components of the project." It is sometimes called the French feedback.

- "Mixed" or "sandwich" feedback, mixing positive and corrective. For example, "I have two comments on your presentation: I liked the way you presented and I think you could improve on the precision of the data." Notice the and instead of but, to make sure corrective and positive feedback are given equal footing. It is sometimes called the American feedback.

- Mentoring feedback or sharing experience. I use this method quite often. I remember a project where I was advising experienced experts of a construction company who were training supervisors. During the training, instead of saying, "After lunch, you should do more activities because people are sleepy," I told them, "Usually, when I run a training session after lunch, I try to get participants involved in activities, so that they stay alert. What do you think?" I found this is a good way to give feedback to experienced experts and managers. It conveys the message while considering ego and respecting their confidence.

In each approach, I often express my feelings (e.g., I worry, I am concerned, I am stressed, I am confused). The way to give feedback is different from country to country, but in all these contexts I found that expressing feelings always softens the message.

It's also important to know how to receive feedback, which is also not always easy to do. I read *Thanks for the Feedback* by Douglas Stone and Sheila Heen[23] on this topic, and it showed me the importance of sticking to facts. That is why, when I end a training session, I don't hand out the usual evaluation questionnaire where we ask the trainees to give marks based on a set of criteria (method, content, trainer, coffee break, etc.). I just ask the two simple questions, and only eventually give some examples of criteria: "Can you tell me what you liked about this training and what I could have done better in this session on topics such as content, method, atmosphere, logistics, etc.?" I might have more to read, but this way, I get valuable input that I can use to improve my future training. I use similarly open questions on feedback forms at the end of a consulting assignment.

I mentioned corrective feedback, but giving positive feedback is essential to motivate. It is often said that French people like me are usually not good at this. Many believe that when people complete the work as expected, then we don't need to congratulate them because it was their responsibility in the first place. I note the difference in mindset when I work with American partners or consultants who are often good at cheering on teams.

4. Sociological analysis of organizations

At the beginning of every consulting assignment, I learn about all the organizations which will be involved in the project. That's when the headache starts: How can we make sure that they will work well together?

There are two kinds of situations – projects for companies and those for governments.

---

23 Stone, D. & Heen, S. (2014) Thanks for the Feedback: The Science and Art of Receiving Feedback Well. Penguin

With a company, I usually deal with two structures: the HR department and their internal client – manufacturing or sales, for instance.

Within large companies with, for example, 20,000 staff, I often find that the large HR department is disconnected from the reality of the other departments. Thus, I hear sentences such as, "This is a demand from head office HR; they don't know what it's like here in the factory."

In all companies, there is often the complaint that managers don't support HR interventions. In my 2023 new year wishes, I remember sending an email to an HR manager with whom I have been working with for many years to wish her great health, a great time with families and friends and … great support from managers for her HR interventions. She replied on the same day, "I really appreciate your wish and hope it will come true!"

When it comes to projects for governments (e.g., creating or improving training institutes, planning vocational training development, creation of programs, etc.), there are, usually, several organizations involved. That can give me more headaches. I have led large vocational training cooperation projects where I had to align the needs of more than 10 different organizations (ministries, training institutes, companies, professional federations from two countries) to make the project successful. That was very challenging.

How can I make all these organizations work together?

Maybe a five-day team-building trip in the jungle would help, but I have not tried (yet).

I use a trusted framework from researchers Friedberg[24] which highlights the importance of answering questions like: What are the needs of the people, as a group or as individuals, in each organization? How do or will they behave based on these needs? What is the power dynamic between them?

This kind of analysis is especially useful when the project includes a public-private partnership where governmental organizations need to agree with companies and federations to jointly create or develop training institutes or programs.

---

24 https://en.wikipedia.org/wiki/Erhard_Friedberg

5. Positive attitude towards others

This essential skill boils down to two personality traits: patience and a sense of humor. If you don't have them naturally, they are difficult to develop.

- ♦ Patience is needed to accept that partners rarely do what we expect them to do. When I get frustrated, I try to calm down by telling myself that if my partners or customers understood what they had to do right away, they wouldn't have hired me.
- ♦ Smiling and having a good sense of humor help create a convivial atmosphere which is a huge help in making a success of a project, especially the hard ones. I once worked with a project director in a ministry for a large cooperation project, and it took me several months to make him smile in our monthly project review meeting. It wasn't for lack of trying. We often face tense situations in our projects, but a fun atmosphere can help to reduce difficulties and build understanding.

6. Computer skills

You might wonder why I'm including such a basic skill?

Consultants are always on a deadline, and they have to write – a lot. Whether it's a report of 20 pages or a 40-slide presentation, they often have to do so without the help of assistants and, most of the time, have never been trained on: 1) how to type quickly on a computer; and 2) how to use basic computer software efficiently.

I remember sitting next to a 65-year-old consultant in a project in Uzbekistan. We were both writing our reports at the same time. He was typing with two fingers, slowly, one word per second.

Why was I typing twice as fast as him? Because 15 years ago, one of my children's high school teachers introduced them, and to me, by extension, to a simple software which taught us how to type with 10 fingers. It changed my life! I still thank him today. I should have learnt it when I started to use computers in 1990. It would have saved me so much time; time I could have used to add value elsewhere while reducing the physical pain that I had in my hands and fingers.

Computer skills include typing at speed and, of course, knowledge of standard office software: Word, Excel, and PowerPoint. When I was team leader of a Thai-French cooperation project, many years ago, I spent a long time writing the final project report for the simple reason that I wasn't able to use Microsoft Word efficiently. I didn't know what I didn't know.

I strongly believe that, as a consultant or trainer, we should follow a five-day course on: 1) how to type quickly; and 2) how to write text efficiently, prepare presentations, and use spreadsheets.

As we can see, these six skills relate to communication.

Figure 14.1: Six skills to keep my job

Conclusion

The six skills identified above are essential for my job, although it does not mean that I have them at the level that I want.

I am sure there are others that I use subconsciously, and I also know that there are others that I should have. I think the most important is to be aware that we, as consultants, need to continuously develop our skills if we want to keep our job and bring real value to our partners and customers.

15. CULTURE SHOCK: MANAGING CROSS-CULTURAL DIFFERENCES

When I go through my LinkedIn connections, I realize the diversity of nationalities and cultures of people I work with.

In the 14 countries where I have implemented HRD projects, I can think of many situations where my French perspective was challenged. For example:

- In Thailand: I have always been puzzled by the way some people communicate and give feedback in an indirect way through gestures, smiles, looks, silence, etc.

- In Vietnam: I was surprised by the contrast between the tension during meetings and the relaxed atmosphere in the after-work dinner with the same people.

- In Sri Lanka: In a meeting with 10 company representatives, I went from confusion to laughter when on my first day on the project, I asked, "Do you have any training needs?" and they all shook their heads from right to left frantically. A head gesture that I knew as "no" meant "yes" there!

- In Uzbekistan: Walking with my local partner through the streets of Samarkand, I was amazed to be discussing the writings of French writers Marcel Proust and Victor Hugo so

far from home, in the middle of an incredible melting pot of
ethnicities.

- ♦ In Laos: I was bewildered when a secretary in the Ministry
of Education spoke loudly to her director, in a very direct
way, far from the typically gentle Southeast Asian way of
communicating.
- ♦ In Morocco: I was amused by the amount of time my
colleagues would spend asking friends about all their family
members (mother, father, sister, grandparents, son-in-law,
etc.) before addressing the topic at hand.
- ♦ In Bangladesh: I have been impressed by the motivation of
teachers that I trained to speak English even when I asked
them to speak Bangla.

We often unwittingly pigeonhole people from different cultures to
make things easy for us. But it's not as simple as that. There are reasons
why people behave in a certain way in a specific situation other than of the
fact they are French, Thai, American, Lao, Vietnamese, Chinese, or from
whichever culture.

Back in 1998, my second assignment in Thailand was in a public Thai
University where I was the only foreigner. During that time, a French professor came to visit. As we were catching up one evening, he asked me, "Do
you have any issues working in Thai culture?"

I replied, "My difficulties at work don't come from differences in the
cultures of France and Thailand, but from the fact that I had never worked
in a public organization before. There are many rules, regulations, and specific behaviors. I think there are more similarities between Thai and French
public universities than between a Thai university and a Thai private
company."

So, yes, when I see my Thai partner Siripan and my French partner Paul
acting differently during meetings or when managing teams, it's not neces-
sarily because they come from different countries with different cultures.

I believe there are four possible reasons why their behavior might differ, and culture is only one of them. A lot of this might seem obvious, but a reminder doesn't hurt as these elements are often overlooked.

1. Siripan and Paul might not have similar personalities. Some people are extroverted, loud, and brash; others are discreet, easygoing, and shy. And it doesn't have anything to do with their culture. It doesn't hurt to remember that not all Thai people are calm and not all French people are hot-tempered.
2. Siripan and Paul might have different needs in the organization. For instance, Siripan is a young Gen Y employee who seeks challenges and promotions at work while Paul is a baby boomer waiting for his retirement, who doesn't want new assignments. Naturally, they will not act the same way nor seek the same goal.
3. Siripan and Paul might have different knowledge and skills, especially in management. I have met French managers who had been living in Thailand for 20 years and knew Thai culture but still encountered a lot of problems in their teams (no trust, no respect, no transparency, staff turnover). I also know French managers who, after only a few months in Thailand, created a good atmosphere within their team. It's all about management skills.
4. Finally, we get to the fourth reason for behavior differences between Siripan and Jean … culture.

Every time I teach a cross-cultural workshop, I start with this introduction to raise awareness among the participants and avoid generalization. This serves as a reminder for myself as well because even after nearly 30 years in Thailand, I still get impatient when I face a behavior from a Thai partner that I think is not suitable.

Having said all that, **cultural differences do exist!**

No matter where you are from, if you're from so-called "Western" countries, in Thailand, you will be a "farhang." I like telling my Thai business partners, "I never met a farhang in my life." They always look at me puzzled, probably thinking, *Is this farhang crazy?* I then tell them, "I have met English, French, Italian, Spanish, and Australian people, and they are all different. Do you think that Indian, Vietnamese, and Thai people are the same?" I always get a clear "no!" ("This farhang is really crazy!"). This is why all my experience of Thai culture means very little when I travel to another Asian country like Bangladesh.

Let's dive into the differences that I have faced for the past 30 years while doing projects in 13 different countries.

My two preferred authors who write about cross cultures are Erin Mayer and Fons Trompenaars.

I like Meyer's culture map comparing **behaviors** in different nationalities through eight axes.[25]

1. *Low- or high-context communication:* Do we need many or a few words when we speak or write emails? For example, the English language has seven times more words than the French.

2. *Direct or indirect feedback:* Thais are well-known for giving indirect feedback, mixing positive and corrective feedback together, or not giving feedback at all to avoid confrontation. Conversely, the French often give direct corrective feedback. You can guess the kind of challenges I have come across over the past 30 years living in Thailand!

3. *Deductive or inductive persuasion:* Do we introduce a new project by explaining the theory, like the French do (deductive approach), or describing examples like the Americans (inductive approach)? I discovered this difference when, as a young, inexperienced engineer, I created a training center on repairing sewing machines in a refugee camp and starting with the theory didn't work.

---

25 Meyer, E. (2014) The Culture Map: Breaking Through the Invisible Boundaries of Global Business. Public Affairs

4. *Leading by equality or hierarchy:* Every day on LinkedIn, you see posts talking about how good leaders should not give the solutions to every problem but coach their team to find solutions by themselves. But this approach, usually found in northern Europe, can be challenging in other countries such as Korea, France, or Thailand. Is the boss very detached or fully engaged with team members?

5. Decision by consensus or top-down: Meyer gives the statistical example that 55% of Italians think the boss should decide, as opposed to 7% of Swedish. These contrasting visions of decision-making will naturally impact the working environment.

6. *Showing trust with paper or words:* In some countries like India or Morocco, asking for a written contract after discussions can be perceived as a lack of trust. This could be explained by the fact that, in some countries, people might not trust the official system (government, laws, etc.) due to the lack of efficiency or corruption so they place greater importance on relationships rather than formal documents.

7. *Disagreeing:* In many Asian countries, saving the other's "face" can be more important than stating that you disagree. My biggest culture shock was when I moved from Morocco, where people tended to openly disagree, to work in Thailand. Newly arrived in 1986, so many times Thai people whom I asked for directions in the streets confirmed to me that I was heading in the right direction just because they didn't want to disappoint me. I had to reboot my understanding and way of expressing disagreement.

8. *Scheduling:* How important is it to be flexible with deadlines? Starting a meeting late or sending a report after the deadline might not be perceived as an issue for some. In countries with rapidly changing weather conditions and chaotic traffic which can cause unavoidable delays, time is relative.

As you can see from the table below, these differences could create a lot of potential issues.

If Paul and Siripan want to work together, I could use the table below to illustrate their cultural differences, although I think that their personal approaches are similar for points 4 and 5.

	Paul	**Siripan**
1	Low context communication	High context communication
2	Direct feedback	Indirect feedback
3	Persuading based on principles	Persuading based on practical examples
4	Leading with equality compared to Siripan	Leading with hierarchy
5	Deciding with a consensual approach compared to Siripan	Deciding with a top-down approach
6	Trusting with paper	Trusting with words
7	Clear message of disagreement	Disagreeing without confrontation
8	Respect of time	Scheduling while keeping flexibility

Figure 15.1: Culture map between a French and a Thai

What are the values that generate these different behaviors? Below, I represent this as a process (I can't help it – it is my engineering background!).

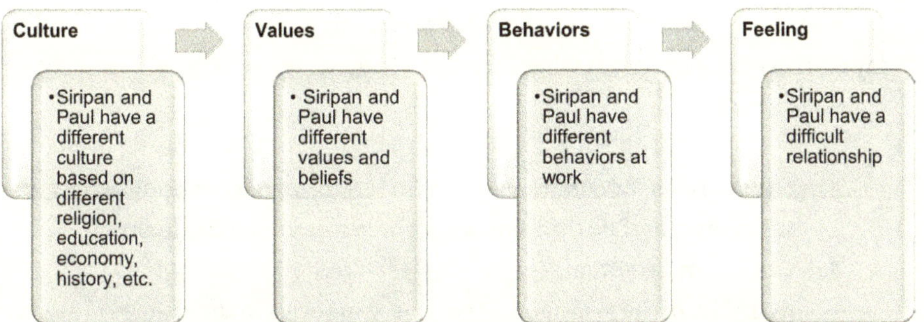

Figure 15.2: How the specificities of culture generate feelings

Trompenaars[26] highlights seven main **values**:

1. *The rule/the person:* Do we give priority to the rule or to personal relations when we are in a difficult situation?
2. *Individualism/group:* Do we prefer being in a group or can we do things alone?
3. *Strong or weak expression of feelings:* Do we express ourselves or hide our feelings?
4. *Separation within life/mixed life:* Do we mix personal and professional lives or not?
5. *Given status/acquired status:* Is our social status acquired by work or attributed by age, diploma, family, etc.?
6. *Sequential time/synchronous time:* Can we multitask (be flexible) or do we need a process (with precise deadlines)?
7. *Shape the world or belong to the world:* Can we shape the world and the environment (including those around us) or are we part of it?

It is getting complicated. So how can we manage these **cross-cultural differences?**

---

26 Hampden-Turner, C. and Trompenaars, F. (2020) *Riding the Waves of Culture: Understanding Diversity in Global Business.* Nicholas Brealey Publishing

Based on ideas I've come up with from reading books on the topic and my own experience, here is what I try to do to generate positive and efficient relationships:

- Set the rules for communication (meeting, emails), reporting, templates, and decision-making processes within the team
- Control my emotions (easier said than done!) and, if not possible, express personal feelings, especially in difficult situations (e.g., "I worry that ...," "I am stressed because ...," "I am not confident with this.")
- Encourage people to express their ideas, ask open questions.
- Speak about cultural differences
- Have regular one-to-ones in addition to team meetings.

Conclusion

When we work with colleagues, subordinates, customers, and partners of different nationalities, first and foremost we must treat everyone as individuals, regardless of their nationality, because we all have different personalities, knowledge, and needs.

Then comes our own culture based on the history, economic development, geographical context, and education system of where we are from. Our background generates various values that explain our different behaviors at work.

Accepting these differences is a daily challenge when we work with other cultures, but following some guidelines, and being self-aware and curious, can help build trust and lead to healthy and productive working relationships.

16. LEADING A TEAM OF CONSULTANTS: CHALLENGING BUT EXCITING

When I lead the implementation of large HRD projects for companies or governments, the teams that I manage often include consultants with a lot of experience in their domain (curriculum design, development of teachers, training equipment, etc.) or with specific knowledge of the country concerned. They are not part of my company; I don't get to select them. They work part-time on the project and, most of the time, I don't even know them before the project starts.

Leading a team of independent consultants is a great adventure. But, like in any great adventure, there are some challenges. Here are six that I have come across.

1. Vision of the project

Each freelance consultant often emphasizes the importance of their domain of expertise, which is normal. They often have a lot of experience. Some of them might have worked in many different countries. They all have their own vision about how the project should be implemented.

I was once involved in a project where the team leader had a different understanding of the project deliverables and plan of activities from mine and the other consultants. He had a different background and experience from us. As we were at the beginning of the project, it was important to secure a common vision. We had lengthy discussions to build a common understanding, which fortunately happened.

In another situation, I led a large team of 10 national and international consultants. We had a quick meeting together at the beginning of the project, then we would meet regularly on site but not altogether. Looking back, I regretted not having spent more time during the first two or three months building a common vision and understanding of the procedures and guidelines. This would have led to the consultants having a better understanding of their personal constraints and how they wanted to implement the project. It would have improved our alignment and motivation. The project achieved the expected results, but we would have probably saved time on explanations and implementation.

2. Constraints

International consultants can have very different needs and constraints.

I have worked with consultants living in countries as different as Malta, Fiji, Australia, and Lao PDR, each with their personal and professional requirements, such as family commitments and commuting time from their home to country of assignment.

They also often work on several projects at the same time, which means that projects might overlap. For example, I generally have around five to seven projects at different levels of implementation at the same time. Therefore, a good work plan must take into account all these consultants' constraints.

3. Vocabulary

HRD has its own jargon, which is almost as difficult to understand as the French language.

I remember intense meetings with a consultant from New Zealand who had a very different approach to defining a competency system. When I arrive in a country that developed its TVET system with German cooperation, the vocabulary and methods used will not be the same as those used in countries that had a long TVET cooperation with France or the UK.

Each expert might bring their own definition and approach for competency, curriculum development, or partnership with companies, and have years of experience to back them up.

4. Cross-cultural differences

In international projects, each consultant brings a different culture lens, which impacts the way they give feedback, delegate, assign jobs, or even communicate.

I once completed a project with a team of Japanese, American, and German consultants, which means that I got to experience three work approaches: one going into details about everything, one always giving very positive feedback, and one highlighting the need to follow procedures (I'll let you decide which is which!).

Another time, I had some meetings with a consultant whose body language consisted of big gestures and speaking loudly, which was the exact opposite of that of our local partners. I could not feel comfortable during these meetings.

5. Communication styles

We may all use emails, reports, or even WhatsApp, but each person has their own way to communicate.

I was once leading a team of French consultants and whenever I sent out emails asking for their intervention or advice, I would receive different answers. One of the consultants, who also was a director of a company, would answer with a very short email and preferred phone calls; another one, who was an education inspector, gave long and precise answers; and the last one, an international project manager, would add his opinions and visions, sometimes on other topics. At first, this gave me a headache, but I learned to be flexible and adapted my communication style, at least to some degree, to match theirs.

Similarly, when I was leading a team of consultants based in ASEAN countries, I would send documents by email, but I quickly understood that the Thai consultant much preferred to receive them through the well-known "Line" chat app. It meant additional work for me, but it made our communication more effective.

6. Document management

We, as consultants, write and receive a lot of documents.

In large projects, you end up with thousands of files. It is essential to have a good classification structure.

Each consultant has their own way of classifying and naming documents, so I can get lost when I have to manage thousands of files. I have encountered all kinds of methods of naming documents: name and date at the end, name only, name of the file and name of consultant, and, worst case, no name but just doc and a number (e.g., doc11).

I spend time trying to make my classification system comprehensive. It helps.

A couple of years ago, a partner from a project which ended a year previously asked me, "Arnauld, can you send me all documents on the project deliverables?" I sent him a hundred files, all precisely classified, right away.

I know that I often get this type of request from my partners, therefore I need to be ready.

Addressing these challenges: **the importance of team rules and one-to-one meetings**

How can I manage all these differences of visions, communication styles, organizations, constraints, and cultures? As all these teams of consultants are, most of the time, spread around in different countries, we need to find simple methods to lead in such a way that everybody feels comfortable. I try to apply these team rules (but do not always succeed):

Time	Take time to discuss the project (vision and modalities of implementation) and review the work plan together
Vocabulary	Build common understanding; discuss, discuss, discuss
Constraints	Consider personal constraints on activities and transportation while planning
Culture	Accept behaviors coming from different cultures
Communication	Set communication mechanisms (reporting, etc.) but adapt them depending on people's personalities
Templates	Provide precise templates for the documents given to customers, but stay flexible for internal documents

**Figure 16.1: Six challenges when leading consultants and
how to address them**

In order to successfully apply these six approaches, I use one key leadership tool that I discovered a few years ago which is increasingly adopted in many organizations for team management.

That is the implementation of regular and systematic weekly/bi-weekly or monthly one-to-one meetings.

I discovered the power of this tool only a few years ago and regret not having used it before in my professional career. For me, they are more important than team meetings.

The main purpose is to build trust with team members by reviewing the four components of performance and retention: motivation, knowledge, resources needed, and individual career plans.

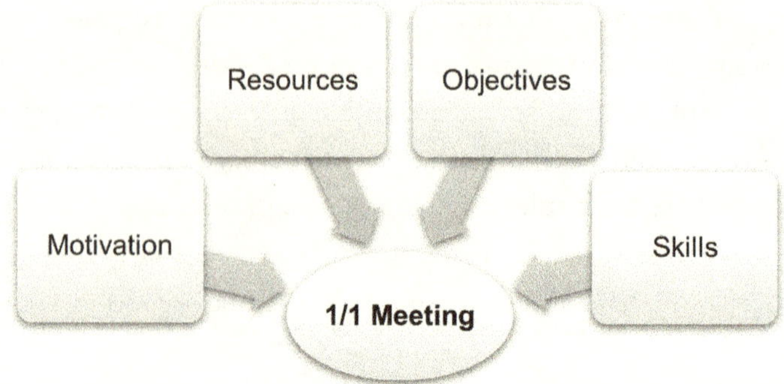

Figure 16.2: One-to-one meeting to review four components

They can last 30 to 60 minutes, depending on the frequency (weekly, bi-weekly, monthly). The team member's past actions/successes/difficulties are reviewed and a plan is formed to overcome challenges, including a discussion on the support and skills development needed. Each leader will have their own approach, but the key concept is to address the needs, feelings, and opinions of the team member.

When I speak about these regular individual meetings in companies where this concept is not implemented, I often get reactions such as, "I do not have time to meet individually with all my team members." If that's the case, I ask how they are able to find the time to delegate, give feedback, coach, motivate, and validate resources needed. In short, I wonder what their definition of leading people is.

I often use the example of a director of factory who had 10 direct reports and was meeting them once every 10 days. For a busy leader like him, this was a clear sign of the importance he gave to this leadership tool.

I remember leading a project where weekly team meetings were planned with both the partner and the company which hired me as team leader. After two months, I asked to change to monthly individual meetings with each team member and only one monthly team meeting. People appreciated it. I was able to get precise information on the vision, feeling, and situation of each team member, especially from the local consultants who were less likely to speak up than the international consultants during our team meeting.

Conclusion

As the proportion of freelance and independent workers increases every year, more and more project managers will face the same kind of challenges that I have come across. I believe that setting up team rules and regular, systematic one-to-one meetings, either face to face or online, are essential to guarantee a shared vision, gain a good understanding of personal constraints, and for taking into account each person's skills, culture, communication style, and way of working.

17. AVOIDING BEING LOST IN TRANSLATION

I rarely use my mother tongue, French. It's a pity, as many foreigners I meet say it's a beautiful language. The problem is, if I were to use it in my everyday work life, I'd probably be the only one understanding what I say. In Thailand, I'm happy to use Thai, but as soon as I go abroad, English is essential.

To navigate in this international world, there are two types of people who are very important for me: 1) "interpreters," who translate spoken language orally; and 2) "translators," who translate written documents.

Translation and interpretation are difficult and essential tasks. In HRD, as well as in other fields, people have their own jargon, with phrases like "competency standards," "blended learning," or "occupational standards" which sometimes have no translation in local languages.

Interpreters and translators I work with fall into two categories:

1. Language specialists who might have little knowledge on the topics I want to present (e.g., HRD)
2. Local HRD experts who know my jargon but might not be so good at English.

Concerning interpretation (oral translation) during meetings, training, and workshops, I share below six tips that maximize the chances of my message being understood the way I meant it (or at least, getting close to it!).

I don't include situations where I have simultaneous interpretations, with one interpreter sitting in a box while the audience has headsets. This has rarely happened to me.

1. Which English language do we speak?

English is spoken by most of my partners, as well as their own language.

In this case, we should all understand each other, right? Well, not always.

When I was working for a Thai university, I invited French professors to come for seminars. That's when I realized that each country has its own version of the English language: Everyone spoke English well, but the French professors spoke "Frenglish" with a vocabulary that Thai participants didn't always understand because they spoke "Thenglish."

Tip: Keep vocabulary and sentences simple and try to use English words and expressions that local partners use and will understand.

2. Lost in translation

I was once in a meeting with the Thai Minister of Education – who spoke in Thai – and representatives of the French Ministry of Foreign Affairs – who spoke in French. The interpreter was disastrous: He didn't use the right names for the organizations nor the right technical terms. The result? Everybody was confused. After 30 minutes of discussion, the Thai Minister said, in English, to his French counterparts, "Maybe we should speak in English." And so they did. I thought that the Thai minister showed great flexibility by proposing this change (more than his French counterpart).

Tip: Before a discussion, meeting, or training, provide the written materials to the interpreters, and review and prepare the topic with them to clarify important words.

3. The art of synthesis

I have been involved in many seminars, meetings, and workshops where an interpreter was needed.

Often, foreign speakers (representatives from foreign governments or international organizations) would speak for five minutes in their own language, using complex sentences of diplomatic and academic language. The interpreter would then take one minute to translate the five-minute speech. The speaker would look at the interpreter doubtfully, clearly expecting more. In this kind of situation, my guess is that the interpreter is probably overwhelmed by the quantity and complexity of the information to translate. Speakers can be too focused on themselves and the important message that they want to convey, but without understanding that if it can't be easily interpreted, their counterpart might understand only a fraction of what they said.

Tip: Use short sentences and simple words, and stop often to let the interpreter speak.

4. We do not know what they do not know

It can be tricky when we are not sure of the level of English spoken by people present. The local partner might tell me something like, "It should be fine, they can understand."

When training of teachers in Bangladesh, I implemented my usual approach of lots of interaction with very few lectures. The evaluation was very positive. When I followed up with individual meetings online, I discovered that some of the teachers could not understand what I was saying without a translator.

The biggest language barrier I have come across was in Turkmenistan, where I had to train 15 participants who all had very different backgrounds. We ended up using four languages: Turkmen, Russian, French, and English. I quickly understood that long lectures were useless, so I focused on individual and group exercises.

Tip: When the people you are training speak a variety of languages, keep lecture time to a minimum and instead generate two-way communication with individual or small groups activities. Ask the interpreter or local partner to walk around, and walk around yourself to check people's understanding and re-explain the content to strengthen the theory taught before.

5. High-speed talk

We have all met Australian, American, or English people who speak as fast as a high-speed train, thinking that everybody understands their accent perfectly. I have an English partner in Thailand, the CEO of a company, whom I really respect because he always speaks slowly and pays attention to this counterpart.

Tip: Speak slowly and give the interpreter time to translate.

6. Double language

In the projects I am involved in, we sometimes organize workshops and seminars. Thus, I give PowerPoint presentations that can, sometimes, be very technical (e.g., about qualification and certification systems). My local partner often tells me to not worry because participants can read English, and I am inclined to believe them. But there can be issues of understanding with the slides and text presented.

Tip: If possible, use two screens, one with the international language (e.g., English) and one in the local language (e.g., Vietnamese). In addition, use pictures and drawings and ask participants to take notes in their language.

To summarize, as a speaker, I must prepare beforehand, focus on my audience, and pay attention to people's reactions: Do they have questions? What are they doing and what are they looking at when I present?

What about the **translation of written documents** (reports, documents, manuals, guidelines, etc.)?

Twenty years ago, if you wanted to translate a 20-page HRD document from English to Vietnamese, you had to find the right translator who also knew the subject. You would hire them, check their work, and ask someone else to review. It took weeks.

How do we proceed, nowadays?

If I want to know the key points of the new vocational education law in Uzbekistan, I get a quick translation using Google Translate. It may be a bit rough and ready, but it will do, although it depends on the language.

But, of course, to produce an official document with specific style standards, I need a precise translation.

Once, I had to produce a 30-page report on the French education system, in Thai, for the Thai Ministry of Education. I was worried that I wouldn't capture its complexity (the French like complex systems and complex words). I wrote the report in English, went on the web, and typed "translation English to Thai." I found some relevant websites, contacted three providers, asked for a trial translation of 10 lines, then selected a company based in the UK that could translate 30 languages. A week later, I received the translation, reviewed it as I can read Thai, was satisfied, and sent it to my counterparts in the Thai ministry. Their main feedback was about the font of characters, but very little about the words used.

Tip: For document translation or proofreading, use the internet.

I summarize these tips on the following page.

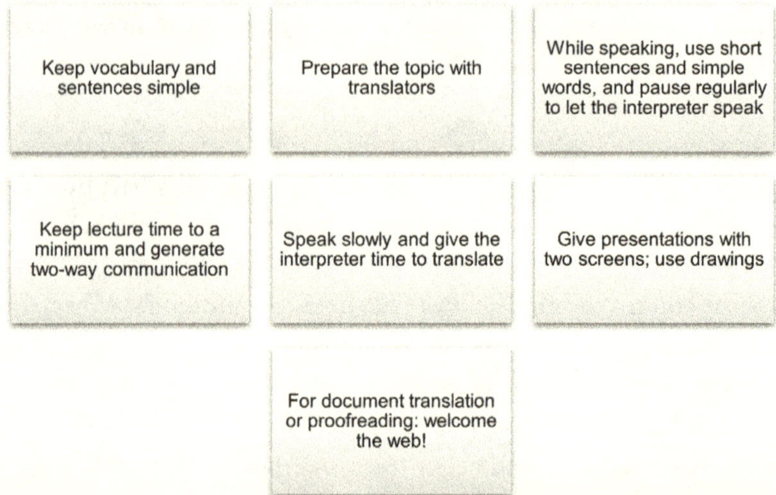

Figure 17.1: Tips to avoid being lost in translation

Conclusion

These are my tips for successful interpretation and translation. I try to adapt them depending on the nature of the work (purpose, duration, preparation time, organizer's resources etc.).

But with the rapid development of artificial intelligence, all these tips might soon be out of date. I will need to closely follow what new opportunities arise to help me communicate the way I want with my partners.

18. FACTS, FEELINGS, AND OPINIONS: THE COMMUNICATION TRINITY

As a consultant, when I analyze a situation, a project, or a system, I am given facts, opinions, or feelings from people at the organization concerned.

These three components are crucial in making my consulting job successful.

We live in a world of **opinions**.

During my projects for companies or governments, people that I interview often say things like, "We have an increase of students in our training centers," "Our leadership training is successful," "It seems that people complain about our performance system," or, "The work of our operators is complex."

These are statements made by managers and government officials who often have a lot of experience. I am willing to believe them. Sometimes too much because, in fact, they do not represent reality.

To get credible information, I ask the same open questions to several people so I am not just relying on the view of one person. But these are still *opinions*. They are subjective and difficult to change. Are they true or not? I can't be sure.

And, to add to the difficulty, these opinions are shaped by the surrounding culture.

Once, the vice president of a German chemical company asked me, "Arnauld, why are our employee engagement scores always higher in our Thai factory than in other countries?"

I told him that I had the same issue. When I evaluate training programs in Thai companies, the satisfaction levels are usually very high, between four and five on a scale of one to five.

While it is a generalization, it is true to some degree that Thai people provide positive feedback because they do not want to hurt people's feelings.

What I need to remember is that I cannot evaluate a situation based on opinions only.

I need **facts**: numbers, statistics, concrete actions, and tangible observations.

Two events in my career strengthened my appreciation for facts.

The first one was in 2010. I was a member of a team of consultants in Lao PDR, tasked with the preparation of a five-year project for the Asian Development Bank to improve the Laotian vocational education and training system.

We had to get a lot of data from reports, documents, and meetings with representatives of the ministries. Our team leader was very experienced, and each time I met him to give my opinion, he would always ask me, "Where is the data and the numbers? What is the proof?" He was right. I had to get the corresponding data. In the final report, each opinion had to be backed up by a chart, table, figure.

Today, when I meet representatives of ministries and managers of companies, I try to focus on numbers, data, and statistics. I say things like, "Show me the statistics of your students and we will check the evolution," "We should calculate the impact of the leadership training on staff turnover and we will see if it is successful," or, "I will count the number of operator tasks and then we can decide if they have too many or not."

The second event was during 2012 and 2013. I obtained two certificates from Pearson (UK) and the ROI Institute (USA) on how to measure the financial benefit and return on investment of any kind of learning and development programs based on precise data collection. Data is collected at five levels, as I mentioned in Chapter 2.

For example, one company selling medicines asked me to measure the return on investment of a program to develop the communication skills of their sales managers.

- ♦ **Level 1:** I collected opinions of the participants on their level of satisfaction with the sessions and converted this into a percentage of satisfaction (number = facts).
- ♦ **Level 2:** I collected opinions of the participants on what they felt they had learned. This gave me a percentage of effectiveness (number = facts).
- ♦ **Level 3:** I collected opinions of the participants and their manager on how they felt the new communication skills could be applied in a set of situations. This gave me a percentage of application (number = facts).
- ♦ **Level 4:** I analyzed the impact on their sales turnover before and after the training (number = facts) and isolated the percentage which came from putting into practice what they had learnt by comparing with other factors. This gave a percentage of income (number = facts).

This is a systematic way of transferring some opinions into data.

I am aware that some numbers based on opinions can be intentionally wrong. I once audited a training institute where the statistics on the number of trainees were just not credible. The heads of departments were hiding the reality of their poor training record to avoid having problems with the financing organization. The problem was that, as I was new in the organization, I had believed some of them.

To conclude, facts and data are important but they can be unreliable, inconsistent, out of date, or just pure fantasy, especially if they are based on opinions.

What about **feeling**?

Tapping into people's feelings is also essential to identify who is driving change in an organization and to propose feasible recommendations.

The difference compared with opinions is that it is not always possible to openly discuss feelings. If someone tells me, "I don't like our performance management system," or, " I worry a lot about the future of our vocational training system," answering "you should like it" or "don't worry" is useless. It is hard to change someone else's feelings.

When I evaluate a colleague's presentation in my public speaking club, Toastmaster, after the speech, instead of giving feedback such as "this was good," "this was not good," "you should do this or that," I start all my sentences with "I": "I was impressed by ..." "I felt connected when you mentioned ..." "I was confused by ..." etc.

I might express my feelings about this presentation 10 times in a three-minute evaluation. The presenter cannot argue with me because I am talking about my feelings while giving valuable information on what was good and what could have been done differently.

In a project that I led, one of my consultants had a lot of experience, so when I did not agree with her presentation, I was careful to use the technique above. Instead of telling her, "This presentation is confusing," I would say, "I worry about what the client will understand from this proposal."

I think that sharing and expressing feelings are important because people are likely to accept them, and it helps in building trust.

Nowadays, in the projects I implement, I try to identify how feelings, opinions, and facts will be collected and used.

For example, in 2019, I evaluated a large skills development project in ASEAN based on a set of precise criteria.

We listed the questions and asked ourselves: Which opinions do we need, and from whom? What facts and data do we need, and from whom? What do people feel about the project?

We implemented 80 individual and group meetings across four countries to get people's feelings and opinions. We reviewed 130 documents, reports, and proposals to get data to confirm or question these opinions.

All these sources of information helped us provide conclusions expressed as opinions. The client did not agree 100% with them, but at least we had collected data to give credibility to our report.

Opinions, facts, feelings, when we connect these three components, then we can get valuable conclusions.

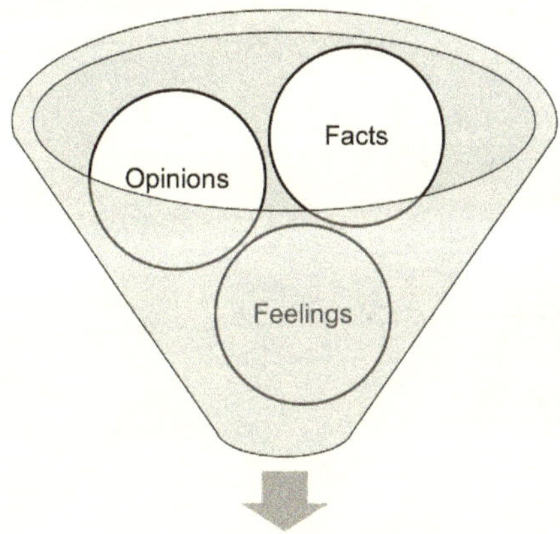

Figure 18.1: Three components to ensure collected data is valuable

Conclusion

Over all these years, I have learned that facts, feelings, and opinions are needed to analyze, audit, or review a situation or context.

They are not easy to get, as they can be hidden, missing, wrong, out of date, or biased; but, together, they can provide the proofs needed for valid conclusions, common visions, and feasible proposals.

19. HOW IT ALL STARTED

In this book, I have shared stories on HRD that I have lived and witnessed during the past 35 years and tried to identify key learnings from these experiences.

I enjoyed thinking back to these projects and situations on topics such as skills development, competency systems, cross-culture, consultancy skills, HRD project management, learning systems, international cooperation, partnerships, personal development, and many more.

How did it start? Where did my passion for HRD come from?

When I was 22 years old, I graduated in France with a master's degree in electrical engineering. A part of me knew that I would not be an engineer all my life, but I also did not know what I really wanted to do, like so many other people at that age!

It took me eight years to find what I wanted to do. At 30 years old, I realized that I was more passionate about developing people than developing technology.

I have met people who found the meaning of their professional life in their 20s and others in their 50s. So, you could argue that I didn't do too badly!

It reminds me of a famous online video of the leadership guru Simon Sinek called "Find Your Why," [27] in which Sinek talks about the importance

---

[27] https://www.youtube.com/watch?v=tF7YLGpOoz8

of finding the purpose, the "why," of our work by reviewing the key events from the past that had a big impact on us.

I have identified four key components that helped me to build my career:

1. When we are young, experiment, experiment, experiment … but with meaning

When I was young, I liked experimenting and tried many things unrelated to engineering. That included volunteering in India for Tibetan refugees, assisting youth in their studies, teaching math for two years in Morocco, creating a training center in a refugee camp in Thailand, etc.

These experiences were not planned. It was not about having a nice CV, a set career path, or earning money. I simply wanted to do something different and meaningful.

At 30 years old, while I was looking for a job as an engineer, I had the opportunity to take my first personality test. I will always remember what the career counsellor said in the debrief, "The results of the tests show that you have the potential and motivation to work in the education and training sector, so … what do you want to do?"

Suddenly, all my past experiments made sense. I decided to switch careers. I refused the offers I had to work as an engineer for the national French railway and a large oil and gas company and instead started to look for jobs in the HRD field.

The following five years were decisive in building the values that would guide my vision of developing people.

I had the chance to work in a French training center with colleagues who promoted and applied the concepts of experiential learning, active listening, and interaction.

I will always remember one small event that happened at this center that demonstrated to me their vision of work. Once, I sent a proposal that was not well written, and my boss reminded me that normally she would review the material beforehand. I told her that I thought it was fine as it was. She did not seem too happy. However, when I finally admitted that I sent it because I wanted to prove that I could write a proposal by myself, suddenly her face changed. She became attentive, actively listening to me talk about my feelings. That is when we started to have a real discussion on my levels of self-confidence and motivation. This center, and these colleagues, built the vision, values, and approach of learning that I have been using throughout my career.

2. It is all about trust

I met several people who believed in me, often more than I did; people who supported my decision to experiment and try new professional adventures. I remember them fondly.

One of them asked me to create a training center for sewing-machine repair in a refugee camp, even though, as you might imagine, my engineering background did not make me particularly well qualified.

Another person recruited me to work in an HRD consulting firm even though I did not have any experience implementing training in companies.

Others selected me to lead Thai-French cooperation projects knowing that I had limited experience in this domain.

And of course, there are all those clients (governments, international organizations, companies) who hired me for assignments outside my comfort zone (and sometimes close to my panic zone!); but I guess they trusted my vision, values, and way of working.

Today, as a consultant, I regularly receive proposals from people asking me to do a job that I think I can't do. Sometimes, I refuse (and regret it later!); other times, I accept and discover that there weren't too many challenges.

3. Be lucid and consistent in knowing who we are

To navigate a career, knowing your strengths is essential. In the past 30 years, I have done four personality tests that have provided me with essential information on my potential and strengths. In addition, I often ask my clients for feedback on what I do well and what I could improve. It is essential, even if it is not always fun to hear or read.

As explained before, sometimes I have doubts that I can do certain jobs even though I probably could. But this knowledge of myself and cautious approach has also helped me say no to jobs that I knew deep down were not for me.

I refused job offers that could have brought me opportunities for professional growth in a large company (e.g., training manager in one of the biggest French weaponry companies), a permanent job with high salary (e.g., head of department in an international consulting firm), or a more impressive title (e.g., director of an international association).

These decisions were easy to make, and I never regretted them.

Knowing what we want to do can take time, but I believe meaningful experimentation, knowing that you are trusted to do the job, consistency of vision, and values which make the most of our personal strengths are essential components.

And, of course, there is ... luck

I was lucky that the person in charge of a project suddenly resigned, which enabled me to take his position in a refugee camp even if I did not have all the qualifications.

Lucky that I met the right people in an unemployment office who advised me to contact a training institute that shaped the rest of my career.

Lucky that there was a budget available for a four-year project in vocational training.

Lucky to have learnt while working with all these refugees, students, volunteers, consultants, trainers, experts, teachers, and managers.

These are the four components that I think were essential to build my HRD career. Hopefully, I will continue to experiment, building trusting relationships, have consistency in my choices, and ... have some luck when I need it.

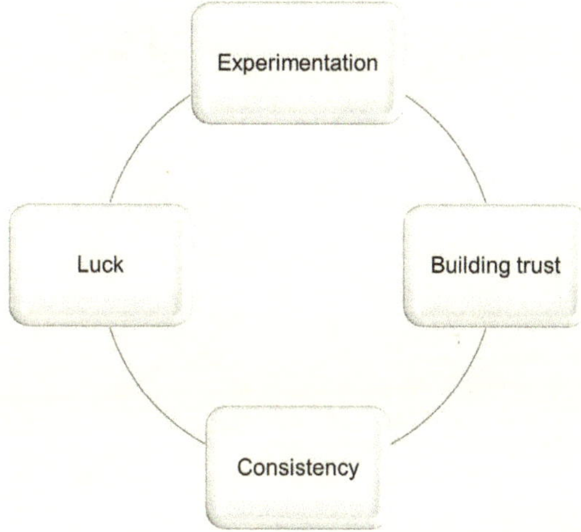

Figure 19.1: Four components in building my HRD career

Conclusion

I was fortunate that I was able to experiment, choose a career path that suited my strengths, skills, and values, and encountered many helpful people on my journey who were willing to take a chance on me. My passion is for HRD because I believe it leads to a better world, but there are many other meaningful pursuits. I hope that my children, nieces, nephews, and many of their generation are lucky enough to find their passion and benefit from the same opportunities as I did.

20. CONCLUSION: KEY LEARNINGS AND CONCEPTS

So, there you have it. Thirty-five years of experience in HRD, filled with joy, stress, uncertainty, fear, passion, disappointment, excitement, and more.

In signing off, I want to sum up the key learnings of these 35 years.

On sharing principles and visions of efficient learning and development

1. Learning methods:

   A hundred years of research can be distilled into nine learning principles: 1) Have a good design; 2) Start with the end in mind; 3) Motivation is essential; 4) Activities must be planned; 5) Learning by doing is the most efficient way; 6) Take into account people's attention span; 7) We need challenges and emotional connections; 8) Spaced repetition avoids us quickly forgetting what we have learnt; and 9) We should use our various senses.

2. Start with the end in mind:

   Evaluation is an essential part of HRD projects, using either a five-level grid (satisfaction, learning, behavior at work, impact, return on investment) or six criteria guidelines (relevance, coherence, effectiveness, efficiency, impact, sustainability).

3. Competency systems:
    Learning is about developing competency in certain skills and
    behaviors. Many systems are available, influenced by different
    countries, but it's not a case of one size fits all, so it is important
    to remain flexible.

4. Self-development:
    As a consultant and trainer, I must keep on learning throughout
    my life, which I do through physical or online training; joining
    associations; seminars and webinars; being a trainer; imple-
    menting project-based reading; sharing with mentors, partners,
    or customers; following e-learning and MOOCs; listening to
    podcasts; and sharing knowledge on social media.

5. Leadership development programs:
    The 70-20-10 model is a highly efficient approach for people
    development, especially for leaders as it enables the integration
    of various learning methods, such as print and mass media-based
    learning, group-based learning, work-based learning, one-to-
    one-based learning and internet-based learning.

6. Digital technologies:
    Nowadays, there is a wealth of learning approaches available on
    the internet which can be either synchronous (online training,
    webinars) or asynchronous (e-learning, MOOCs, podcasts/
    videos, mobile learning, and reinforcement). But artificial
    intelligence is the new disruption.

7. Online training:
    To overcome the challenges of transferring physical training
    online, I share some tips plan small sessions, stand in front of
    the screen instead of sitting, use a dedicated light and head-
    phones, constantly interact, split participants into small
    breakout rooms, make slides interactive, and use the various
    supporting apps at your disposal.

On how to implement HRD systems

8. **Conditions to successfully transfer HRD systems:**
   It is easy to know what to do but much more difficult to know how to implement a new system and make it sustainable. To do so, I assess which components can be transferred to an organization or need to be simplified. Finding the right counterpart in the local organization I work with is essential. I adopt a three-phase approach to change behaviors: 1) transfer system; 2) train; 3) monitor to support implementation, using various methods to reduce resistance to change grouped into four levels: information on the change, education to develop skills, participation of the people concerned, and obligation with enforcement.

9. **Future-proof production operators and workers:**
   In an age of huge disruption in the workplace, when we know that millions of jobs will disappear or change, we must provide opportunities for our young people by strengthening apprenticeship systems and building the career path of existing production operators and workers by designing classification and upskilling programs. Success will depend on the motivation of both companies and workers.

10. **Real and potential customers:**
    There is such a variety of customers I need to adapt to: long-term ones who hire me for my full scope of expertise or for just one of my skills; those with whom I completed one project and hope to work with again in the future; those I work with once who never contact me again; and then there are multiple cases of prospects who could become customers if I play my cards rights.

11. **Matching demands and needs:**
    As a consultant, I often see a mismatch between the demands and needs of customers or partners: I shared seven types of situation. But I can build common understanding by negotiating, asking open questions (eventually the same ones to different people), getting data, and meeting people individually more than in group settings.

12. **Partnerships between a company and an institute:**
    In many countries, companies want to partner with education or training institutes. I use six steps to ensure that the company succeeds: review socio-economic disruption, define the target group, describe the kinds of skills needed, address the issue of recognition, review the supply (education and training institutes), and, finally, take decisions within nine possible kinds of cooperation.

13. **Vocational education improvement:**
    How can we implement large cooperation projects to support the development of national vocational education systems? There are four kinds of implementation: national reform, a local intervention, supporting one institute, and advising at national or local level. But, to succeed, certain conditions are needed for each of these four approaches.

On knowledge, skills and capacities needed to successfully implement these systems

14. **Consultant skills:**
    As my job is to develop people skills, I need to ensure that I myself have a set of key skills: asking questions to understand the need, motivating through powerful public speaking, giving positive and corrective feedback, analyzing the relations between various organizations, using computers efficiently

to optimize time, and, last but not least, displaying a sense of humor and patience.

15. **Cross cultural relations:**
    To successfully live and work in a cross-cultural environment, I need to get to grips with the variety of behaviors that others might have and the values that will generate them, using certain guidelines to aid my understanding. Setting up rules of communication, trying to control emotions, sharing openly with people, and having regular one-to-one meetings will encourage smooth working relationships.

16. **Leading teams of consultants:**
    Leading a team of independent consultants is a great adventure, but it can be challenging. To smooth the path and ensure the team work together, I must spend time building a common vision, consider their personal constraints, understand their cultural differences, communicate effectively, especially through one-to-one meetings (adapting to different styles), and make templates and guidelines available.

17. **Language:**
    Working with interpreters, I try to apply basic rules like keeping vocabulary and sentences simple, using English words and expressions that local partners can understand, providing the written materials to the interpreters before and during interpretation, or stopping often to let the interpreter speak. In training sessions, I run individual or small group activities instead of giving lectures, I speak slowly, and I display screens in English and the local language during presentations, when possible.

18. **Facts, feelings, and opinions:**
    As a consultant, to understand the situation and context, I must get facts (statistics, data, numbers), ask for opinions from all kinds of people, and identify feelings of the persons concerned.

All of these elements are important and need to be collected to build a set of proofs that generate reliable conclusions.

19. Reflecting on how all started

For 35 years, I have been able to do this work, which I love, because I have experimented out of my comfort zone, I was trusted by others, and I remained consistent on my values and what I want. Luck has made the difference at key moments. I wish the same for the readers of this book.

And that's it, I have given you all my tips and tricks. Sometimes they work, and sometimes they don't. I don't always manage to follow everything that I have written in this book.

But learning is a never-ending journey. A decade from now, no doubt much will have changed and I will have new learnings to share with you.

Who knows, there might be a second edition of this book ...

Printed in the USA
CPSIA information can be obtained
at www.ICGtesting.com
LVHW090223070224
771109LV00001B/131